God's Creative Gift—
Unleashing the Artist in You

God's Creative Gift— Unleashing the Artist in You

Bible Studies to Nurture the Creative Spirit Within

Jody Thomae

WIPF & STOCK · Eugene, Oregon

GOD'S CREATIVE GIFT—UNLEASHING THE ARTIST IN YOU
Bible Studies to Nurture the Creative Spirit Within

Wipf & Stock
An Imprint of Wipf and Stock Publishers
199 W. 8th Ave., Suite 3
Eugene, OR 97401
www.wipfandstock.com

ISBN 13: 978-1-62032-615-2
Manufactured in the U.S.A.

Dedicated to
Dale, Madelyn, & Evan

Contents

Acknowledgments

Jody Wishes to Thank . . .

Dale—for believing in me. I love you, always and in all ways. Need I say more?

Madelyn Ruth, "Magnificent Companion"—for your patience. You are indeed a magnificent friend to all. I pray that as you grow in your relationship with Christ, you will find him to be the most magnificent friend you could ever ask for. I love you and am so proud of the woman you are becoming.

Evan Godfrey, "Young Warrior for God's Peace"—for your care. My gentle, kind warrior who strives for peace for everyone around him. You bring me and others great joy. May you always walk in *His* beautiful destiny for your life. I love you, mighty one. Be strong and courageous.

Dad & Mom—for allowing me to live a life of whimsy, creativity, and make-believe. Dad, I miss you, and I hope God lets you read this from heaven. Mom, as you played the piano in our living room, and I listened from my bedroom, you became my first example of a Christian artist. You are the most courageous and beautiful woman I know.

Kim, Lynn, & Sue—for encouraging me and walking alongside me through this lengthy project. You all inspire me to be more than I think I can be, and I love you for your thoughts, insights, and ideas, but most of all, your friendship.

Sarah—for making me submit. Not sure where this project would be without you? I love being creative with you.

Acknowledgments

Aaron, Alison, Amy, Beth, Brittany, Dave, Eric, Heather, Jeremy, Jillian, Kati, Kim, Kristin, Laurie, Lenore, Lydia, Nate, Pat, Rachel, Shana, Shelbi, Sherry, Tony—for worshiping with me over the years in ministry. A part of each of you is in these pages.

Dr. Terry Wardle—for your guidance, direction, and care, and for starting me on my healing journey. This project is very much a result of that journey. I thank you for listening to the voice of the Healer.

Dr. Tim Crow—this book started in your class with my study of the symbolic acts of the prophets. Thank you for allowing me to explore the creative side of God.

Dr. JoAnn Watson & Dr. Wendy Corbin-Reuschling—for your direction, encouragement, and guidance.

Foreword

KIM IS AN ENGINEER by education. Although she always loved to sing and was in her high school show choir, she left that part of her life behind as she ventured to college, majoring in engineering because she was "good in math and science." She now sings on the worship team and helps with drama and dance at our church. She wouldn't call herself an artist, and she doesn't necessarily consider herself highly creative. Yet she can remember every lick of choreography, and when she sings, she has an intuitive sense of her role as she helps lead worship.

Laurie is an art teacher. She has also danced with me at our church and has an innate sense of movement from her days of gymnastics in her youth. While she doesn't have time in her life to paint for herself, she painted the most amazing murals for our Vacation Bible School. She also has a beautiful soft spot in her heart for children that others would overlook or find troublesome or annoying. She knows the arts have power to give them a voice.

Bobby is the artistic director of a regional ballet company. He works in a secular market, but when he dances he reflects both the glory and the artistry of God, bringing the sacred to the secular. He is open about his faith and participates in regional worship dance workshops, but the majority of his time is spent dancing with people of a variety of faiths and beliefs. God has called him to reflect his radiance in a field that is otherwise void of God's light.

This book is for all the Kims, Lauries, and Bobbys in our churches. For anyone who's ever sewn a pair of angel wings on a leotard or has created beautiful costumes of intricate detail. For those who paint backdrops for Christmas plays and those who paint for a living. For those who write secret letters to God in their journals or who write published works all about God. For those who sing in small choirs in rural churches and for those who write, record, and share their music with people around the world.

You have a gift. You may not realize it, but you do. For God has placed in you a gift of creativity. While some people have figured out a way to make a living with this gift, many others give it away freely and voluntarily. Still others slough off their creativity as nothing. Wherever you find yourself on the continuum, your innate creativity is a gift from God. As you begin to consider this notion, two thoughts are of utmost importance here: first, our God is a creative God; second, you are made in his image. Understand? You are made in the image of a creative God. He has placed his creative spirit within you as a gift.

And as the saying goes, our gift is a gift that keeps on giving.

Artists and creative types (or simply "creatives") see things where others do not. We often find meaning in what others deem insignificant or unimportant. We look at the spider weaving its web and find God in the intricacy of it. We look at the face of the person with whom we're sharing coffee and conversation, and if we look and listen hard enough, we see and hear God. By the very nature of our gift, we see and we hear things that others overlook and disregard. Then as we call these things to attention so others can see and hear what God is trying to reveal, we pass this gift on to others. Our gift is that God's image is revealed through us. Our gift is that God's glory is made real through us.

So our gift is twofold. It is a gift of creativity given to us by our Creator, and it is a gift that is given to others as we reveal the Creator to a world desperately in need of his revelation.

As creative people in the church, we've often been overlooked. Unless we sing or play an instrument, we find it difficult to fit in or understand how our creative gifts can be used in our religious settings. Frankly, the church doesn't quite know what to do with us. Encumbered by tradition, dogma, and "we've always done it this way," the church squelches the creative spirit that dares to share an idea that is outside the comfort zones of our four walls of custom, ritual, ceremony, and practice.

But now, it is time to unleash the gift of God's artistry within. It is time that we know the precious gift within us and the beautiful gift we have to offer. Made in his image, his creative Spirit dwells within us all. Set free the creative! Let loose the artist! Release God's Spirit in our lives, in our churches, and in our world!

Preface

"I believe in the individuality of the human soul. We're each artists,
along with God, in its creation. Meister Eckhart believed that an artist
isn't a special kind of person but that each person is a special kind of
artist. Think of it: you're your own special kind of artist. Your soul is
your canvas, your flute, your poem. And you paint it, play it, and write
it as every true artist does—in unique collaboration with God."

—SUE MONK KIDD, *WHEN THE HEART WAITS*

Books written with Christian artists and creatives in mind are few
and far between. As a creative person growing up in the church, for me
Rory Noland's *Heart of the Artist* was the one and only go-to book in this
genre for decades. More recently there have been more entering the market
as artists realize they have something valuable to share with others. Yet of
those books, none are written as an in-depth devotional guide that takes the
artist through a series of Bible studies to aid in their spiritual development.

Originally I had planned to write a book specific to the area of sacred/
liturgical dance, but as I began to write I found that much of what I wanted
to say applied to all areas of the arts. I began to see that movement was as
much a part of the visual arts as painting and that painting was as much a
part of dance as movement. I began to see the creative and the Creator in
the architect and the weaver, the singer and the songwriter, the sculptor and
the welder.

God opened my eyes to see that the "artist" is so much more than just
those who work in the area of fine arts, and that there is an artist inside each
of us longing to express itself in our creative endeavors. I began to see inspiration for craftsmen and women of all types of mediums and materials.
I saw silversmiths, woodworkers, and jewelry makers who worked at their

craft as if for the Lord. I met video editors, filmmakers, graphic designers, and photographers who captured beautiful, sacred moments in a way that was divinely artistic. I realized there are engineers, dental hygienists, and computer programmers who happen to be very creative. I met sound techs and tech crews who saw a vision and did all they could to help clear the way for others to see.

I realized that sometimes we simply need help opening our eyes to see the artist within each of us. I also knew that God wanted to inspire all of these people, not simply because they were creative, but because they were made in his beautiful image.

So, this project is designed as an in-depth devotional Bible study that focuses on the artist within each of us. It is designed to help you draw your creativity and inspiration from a Deeper Source. Each chapter is comprised of two sections: the beginning of each chapter is intended as a summary of the subject area, and the end of each chapter has a series of five devotionals that dig deep into various Bible passages related to that subject area. The first chapter looks at Genesis 1 and the role of *Creation* and creativity in the life of the artist. The second chapter looks at John 1 and the role of *Incarnation* in the ministry of the artist. Chapter 3 begins to explore the idea of a *Theology of Beauty*. Chapters 4 and 5 cover, respectively, the *Priestly* and *Prophetic Roles* of the artist. Chapters 6 and 7 will focus on the creative process as a way of *Prayer* and *Seasons* in the spiritual life of the artist.

It is my desire that this project is not merely informational, but transformational in nature. It is designed with a holistic mindset that encompasses the person as a whole—heart, soul, mind, and strength (Mark 12:30)—and not as a fragmented, fractured individual comprised of various aspects of being.

Fellow Ashland Theological Seminary graduate Emily Pardue is a minister, dancer, and leader of dancers. She once said something that has stayed with me as I have grown in my own ministry:

A dancer cannot dance what she does not know.

These words are so very true. One cannot pretend to be the voice of God through movement, or any other form of artistry, if one does not know the voice of the One for whom he or she speaks.

As creative artists, we must enter into the word of God on a regular basis in order to first hear that voice for ourselves. We must study, know, and memorize his word so that we can recognize his voice among all the other voices in this world.

We must know the choreographer of our steps . . .
    the designer of all our designs . . .
        the creator of our creative heart, soul, mind and body . . .
        the author and perfecter of our faith.
        And we must know Him intimately.

It is my prayer that these subjects and their related devotional studies will help the creative Christian and artist know the Master of All Creators more intimately.

Each chapter is designed as a resource that will aid in the understanding of the person who uses the creative arts in worship, as well as those who use their art form and creativity as a way to bring light to a world of darkness and despair. It is also designed to help you draw closer to God through your creativity. I pray that you will "embody" these ideals in order to understand why every action, movement, and step; every vocal inflection, mime, or character portrayed; every note, harmony, and song; every brushstroke, color, and hue; every pinch of clay and turn of the wheel; every word, metaphor, or literary device; every graphic, photo, angle, and frame; every choice you make as a creator of art, has meaning—for the audience, the artist, and most importantly, the Divine Artist who is glorified through our humble creative offerings.

Prelude: The Beginning of Things

Genesis 1 and John 1

In the beginning . . .

In the beginning . . .

In . . .

In . . .

the . . .

the . . .

beginning . . .

beginning . . .

In the beginning . . .

In the beginning God created the heavens and the earth.

In the beginning was the Word.

In the beginning God created the heavens and the earth.
And the earth was formless and empty,
darkness was over the surface of the deep,
and the Spirit of God was hovering over the waters.

In the beginning was the Word,
and the Word was with God, and the Word was God.
He was with God in the beginning.
Through him all things were made;
without him nothing was made that has been made.
And God said, "Let there be light," and there was light.
God saw that the light was good,
and He separated the light from the darkness.
God called the light "day," and the darkness he called "night."
And there was evening, and there was morning—the first day.

In him was life, and that life was the light of men.
The light shines in the darkness,
but the darkness has not understood it.

Water and sky.
Through him all things were made.

Earth and sea.
Without him nothing was made that has been made.

Day and night; sun, moon and stars.
Through him all things were made.

Creatures of the sea, of the air, and of the land.
Without him nothing was made that has been made.

And God saw that it was good, and God blessed them.
Then God said, "Let us make man in our image, in our likeness . . ."
So God created man in his own image,
in the image of God he created him;
male and female he created them.
In him was life, and that life was the light of men.
The light shines in the darkness,
but the darkness has not understood it.
The true light that gives light to every man
was coming into the world.

God saw all that he had made, and it was very good.
He was in the world,
and though the world was made through him,
the world did not recognize him.

Then God said, "Let us make man in our image, in our likeness . . . "
He came to that which was his own,
but his own did not receive him.

So God created man *in his own image,*
Yet to all who received him,
he gave the right to become *children of God*

In the image of God he created him;
male and female he created them.
—children born not of natural descent,
nor of human decision or a husband's will, but born of God.

And God blessed them.

God saw all that he had made, and it was very good.

The Word became flesh and made his dwelling among us.

We have seen his glory, the glory of the One and Only,

who came from the Father, full of grace and truth.

In the beginning . . .

In the beginning . . .

In . . .

In . . .

the . . .

the . . .

beginning . . .

beginning . . .

In the beginning . . .

In the beginning God created the heavens and the earth.

In the beginning was the Word, and the Word became flesh

and made his dwelling among us.

one

Creation, Creativity, & the Artist

"In the beginning, God created . . ."

When I was a little girl, I spent countless hours putting on "shows." I would gather all the neighborhood girls (three or four), and we would work tirelessly until we had a production worthy of our parents' viewing (somewhat like cheesy karaoke). Just the right songs were selected (from vinyl records) and choreography developed for each (picture lots of swinging arms and clapping). We wore fringed tops (cut-up old t-shirts), adorned with (magic marker) designs and shiny (glued-on) sequins. We "printed" (wrote out multiple copies of) programs and sent out hand-made invitations (on lined notebook paper). Finally, on opening day (two days later), my mom graciously supplied a lavish spread (of cookies and coffee) to all the parents (five or six) filtering into our living room. When the curtain (bed sheet) fell, the show was met with abundant applause (our parents were so kind).

The ironic thing? I'm still doing much the same thing today.

See, there in the basement of my childhood home, I was simply doing what God had designed me to do. With joy, pleasure, and purpose, I created from a mysterious place of child-like wonder and fascination. I drew from a creative well deep in my spirit, placed there by God's Spirit—the same Spirit that hovered over the waters of the earth before life began.

The Beginning of Things

Have you ever stopped to consider the opening words of our Bible? "In the beginning, God created . . ." In the very beginning of time and of the universe as we know it, *God created!* In the first record we have of God's activity, we find him in the process of creating. He wasn't thinking or reading or contemplating or learning—he was creating! As an artist or creative person, that should not only empower you, but also make you ecstatic! As we ourselves "begin" this study, we want to turn first to our Creator. So we will begin here in Genesis to consider what creation has to do with the artist or creator (small c) in relationship to the Master Artist and our Loving Creator (big C).

You might be saying to yourself: "Yes, I understand: God created, and so too must we." Simple, right? Yes, but can we dig deeper? Let's think about creativity in light of a creative God who is the source of our creativity. Some artists talk about "divine inspiration" and how the Holy Spirit guides them as they create. Some artists just create and watch to see what happens. Some artists think, plan, and contemplate for weeks, months, or even years before they begin a work of art. It begs the question: Where does our creativity originate?

Origins of Creativity

German theologian Paul Tillich (1886–1965) spent much of his life considering religion in its relationship to culture and art. He was often criticized for his abstract way of thinking, but his thoughts on art and creativity demonstrate their importance to his spiritual life. Among the myriad of ideas on creativity, he discussed the differences between *originating* creativity, *sustaining* creativity, and *directing* creativity.[1]

Originating creativity is that which can only be possessed by God and originates from God himself. Theologians often call this *creatio ex nihilo* (creating something out of nothing), and restrict it to the original act of creation itself. *Sustaining* creativity is the ongoing support of creation and all that it entails. It is God's creativity in the very present moment through us his creatures. Finally, *directing* creativity encompasses the future "actualization" of creation in all its possibilities. In this sense, it has an eschatological dimension in that all of creation is purposed towards fulfillment of God's coming reign in his kingdom here on earth and in heaven through his son, Jesus Christ. We see this coming from the writings of the apostle Paul, who states that "all of creation has been groaning" in anticipation of its future glory when "creation itself will be liberated from its bondage to decay and brought into the glorious freedom of the children of God" (Rom 8:21–22).

According to Tillich, all of humankind's creativity is rooted in God and the Holy Spirit. For true creativity, a person's spirit must be open to God's

Spirit or no true creativity occurs. If the unbeliever falls into something creative it is only through his or her openness to the Spirit and through the prevenient grace of God.

We see these ideas echoed by others. Dutch Neo-Calvinist Abraham Kuyper (1837–1920) wrote: "God is the Creator of everything; the power of really producing new things is his alone, and therefore he always continues to be the creative artist."[2] He and his contemporaries believed that the artist's role wasn't simply to mimic nature's beauty, but to use the material substance of this world to bring forth new avenues of beauty that "anticipate heaven and recall paradise lost."[3] Quaker missionary and teacher Thomas Kelly adds these eloquent thoughts:

> It is curious that modern psychology cannot account wholly for flashes of insight of any kind, sacred or secular. It is as if a fountain of creative Mind were welling up, bubbling to expression within prepared spirits. There is an infinite fountain of lifting power, pressing within us, luring us by dazzling visions, and we can only say, The Creative God comes into our souls. An increment of infinity is about us. Holy is imagination, the gateway of Reality into our hearts.
>
> . . . The song *is put into* our mouths, for the Singer of all songs is singing within us. It is not we that sing; it is the Eternal Song of the Other, who sings in us, who sings unto us, and through us into the world.[4]

Modern day theologian Jeremy Begbie has built a contemporary theology of the arts on the foundation laid by others. Begbie invites us to be "secretaries" and "priests of creation."[5] He states: "In humankind, creation finds a voice. . . . Through the human creature, the inarticulate (though never silent) creation becomes articulate."[6]

Creativity from Another Source

There is a definite sense that the work that flows from our hands, the music that pours from our instruments or voices, the dance that moves through our bodies, the words that are composed through our pens, are not our own. They are from Another who still longs to speak *to* his creation *through* his creation. When we seek to separate our art from the source of our Creative Center in order to understand its meaning, structure, form, or context, we are in danger of silencing the Creator's voice.

According to composer Igor Stravinsky, the creator, the Creator, and the creative process are inseparable: "The very act of putting my work on paper, of, as we say, kneading the dough, is for me inseparable from the pleasure of creation. So far as I am concerned, I cannot separate the spiritual effort from the psychological and physical effort; they confront me on the same level and do not present a hierarchy."[7] I can recount many times in the creative process when God's Spirit seemed to break in and interrupt me, reminding me of how he loves and forgives me. In those encounters, I realize the truth he is revealing to me is the same truth he wants to reveal to *all* his children.

Have you ever been caught by surprise in the midst of your creative process? As if something from beyond you was flowing through you without thought or concentration? *That*, I believe, is the Creator using you—your hands, your body, your voice, your imagination—as the conduit through which he speaks and appears to his creation and created. You become his mouthpiece, his body, his hands, his feet, his heart.

It's All Good

Over and over God affirms the goodness of creation. Look at the pattern of creation in Genesis 1:

> And God said, "Let . . ."
> And it was so.
> And God saw that it was good.

God speaks, God takes action, and God sees and proclaims that what he has done is good. In this world of pain, destruction, injustice, and evil, we have a tendency to focus on the fallenness of creation. And some go so far as to say that the arts should be banned from our churches because they are "of this world" (material) and not of God (spiritual). But ultimately, God has declared that his creation is good (material and spiritual together)! As creators ourselves, we must reclaim the goodness of creation.

In the words of Richard Foster, "God loves matter. In his original creative acts God affirmed matter again and again, declaring it good at every point along the way. We, therefore, should take the material world quite seriously; it is the 'icon' of God, the epiphany of his glory. We must not dismiss material things as inconsequential—or worse yet, as genuinely evil."[8] Begbie agrees and further argues "for a recovery of a deeper sense of our embeddedness in creation, and of the physicality of artistic creation; the rootedness of art in substance, in the human body, in stone, pigment, in the twanging of gut, the blowing of air on reeds."[9] Later, he also submits that "art is best construed as a vehicle of interaction with the world: a work of art is an object or happening *through which* we engage with the physical world we inhabit, and *through which* we converse with those communities with whom we share our lives."[10] As co-creators,[11] working in cooperation with God's creative activity, we must work towards reclaiming, recovering, and reinterpreting the world around us in relationship with those in whom our lives touch, if even in the slightest measure.

Begbie proposes a world in which order has its roots in the Divine and disorder comes from the fallen nature of the world in which we live. Within that world of order and disorder, he suggests the following for the creative people in our midst:

- *Discovery*

- *Respect* (vs. domination and manipulation)

- *Development* (a bringing forth of new forms of order out of what we are given at the hand of the Creator)

- A *redeeming of disorder* (mirroring God's redeeming work in Christ)

- Creativity set in a *corporate* context (recognizing that self-fulfillment is discovered only in relationship).[12]

Within this relational context, the artist has a role of "setting the record straight"—of forming order out of chaos and disorder. Do we see ourselves in this way? Further, do we understand the importance of this role?

What others see as painful or ugly or evil can and should be re-examined in light of the goodness of God's creation, the redemption of that creation through Christ's death and resurrection, and the ultimate reclamation of all creation when God takes back all the enemy has sought to kill and devour, and when, as for John, a new heaven and a new earth stands before our eyes (Rev 21:1). The atrocities of human trafficking bring to light stories of courage, perseverance, and rescuers who stand defiant in the face of this evil. The plight of the malnourished, thirsting, and starving forces us to look beyond our own selfishness to the needs of others and paints beautiful portraits of sacrifice and compassion.

When my father died several years ago, the acts of kindness, care, and support for our family came from some of the most unexpected places and revealed a much deeper sense of God's goodness—all through the actions of others. As co-creators with God, we must help others reinterpret this world and its disorder in light of his beautiful, redeeming love, so that his glory can be revealed and be made known. When God placed Adam and Eve in the garden and made them caretakers of his creation, he was in fact involving all of us in the continuation of his creative work. Moreover, speaker and author Trevor Hart contends that our creative work is an "unconditional obligation" and a "proper response" to work as co-creators with our Creator.[13]

Created in His Image

All of this finds its roots in another idea that originates in this first chapter of Genesis. We find this in verses 26–27: "Then God said, 'Let us make man in our image, in our likeness.' . . . So God created man in his own image, in the image of God he created him; male and female he created them." What does it mean that we are made in the image and likeness of our Creator and how does that relate to us as creators ourselves? Leading up to these verses we see that the plants and animals are all created "according to their kind." However, man and woman were created in God's image.

The Hebrew word for "image" here is *besalmenu*. It means resemblance, likeness, a representative figure, or a shadow or illusion, and it carries with it the notion that we are not God, but we are *like* God. It is repeated again in Genesis 5:1–3 where we see a repetition of man being created in God's image and then also Seth, the son of Adam, being born in the image of his earthly father Adam. Just as Adam resembles his Heavenly Father, Seth resembles his earthly father. Like DNA passed through family lines, Adam was created in the image of God, and that image was passed down through his earthly flesh and blood to his own son, Seth.

We too share in this familial heritage. I am often told that I resemble my father. How much more then do I resemble my Father in heaven? It is interesting to note that the Hebrew phrase we translate as "in God's image" is only seen one more time in the positive when God re-establishes his covenant with Noah after the great flood, and we are commanded not to shed the blood of another because the other is made in the image of God (Gen 9:6). All other references to "image" in the Old Testament are negative in that they refer to idols and false, graven images.

Old Testament scholar Hermann Gunkel points out that the author of Genesis takes great pain in establishing "the great value of humans."[14] In previous verses we see God speaking as such: "Let there be . . ." and "Let the water . . ." and "Let the land . . ." (1:3, 6, 9, 11, 14, 20, 24). Then, to signal something new and different, God's words change: "Let us make man in our image . . ." (v. 26). The "us" and "our" in this verse contributes to the Christian doctrine of the Trinity. And while it has been the topic of much debate, it is certain that God is sharing this creative process with those around him. The author of Genesis enforces our unique nature in that humanity is given a blessing and dominion over all creation. Finally, God proclaims that his last day of creating is "*very* good" (1:31, emphasis added). We are not just good: we are *very* good! We are the pinnacle of creation—made to look like our Father, to resemble him, to be blessed by him, and to care for all that he has given us.

Think of all the times we have sought to define ourselves by the world's standards. As artists we often feel misunderstood or unappreciated. Just today, on a study break getting a cup of coffee at the local shop, the conversation turned to the subject of my study. "I am writing about creativity and the artist," came my reply.

"Oh," came the blank, almost dumbfounded response.

I chuckled as I walked to my car. "No one gets an artist," came my thought as I shook my head.

Yet, does it matter? Does it matter that as a co-creator with God that what I do is understood by others? Isn't what I am more important?

Identities Shaped by Image

How can our identities be shaped by the knowledge that we are created in the likeness/image of our Heavenly Father? That we are his children? That we share a family resemblance to the Creator of the Universe? Lay hold of that thought! We are not just another person in the masses of humanity. Like individual and unique snowflakes, who we are blankets this earth in sparkling beauty, allowing the earth to rest before it springs forth in glorious splendor. As a dancer, I am told by the world's religious standards that what I do should not be allowed in our churches because our bodies are sinful and shameful. Yet God tells me that I am "*very* good" and that he is pleased with the masterpiece of his creation.

Ephesians 2:10 tells me that "I am God's workmanship, created in Christ Jesus to do good works, which God prepared in advance for me to do" (paraphrase). The word "workmanship" is translated from the Greek *poiema*, from where we derive the word poem. I am God's poem—his written creation that speaks of his love, beauty, and glory! As artists and creative types, we must ignore the blank, dumbfounded stares of the world. We must respectfully embrace that we are the pinnacle of creation, that we are his masterpiece and the creation of his hands. We must humbly recognize that he has created us for a purpose, and that purpose is to represent him in this world of disorder, to make his name known throughout the earth, to speak and to act on his behalf, and to radiate his glory for creation to see and understand.

In the words of Eugene Peterson:

> The Genesis stories of creation begin with "heaven and earth," but that turns out to be merely a warm-up exercise for the main event, the creation of human life, man and woman, designated "image of God." . . . If you want to look at creation full, creation at its highest, you look at a person—a man, a woman, a child. The faddish preference for appreciating creation in a bouquet over a squalling baby, for a day on the beach rather than rubbing shoulders with uncongenial neighbors in a cold church—creation with the inconvenience of persons excised—is understandable, but it is also decidedly not creation in the terms it has been revealed to us.[15]

While I must counter that we can and should appreciate the beauty of creation as found in nature (for it too was created by God), I am also in complete agreement that the fullness of creation is indeed found in humanity.

I admit: I am amazed at the beauty of a praying mantis and its ability to sit quietly and, despite its size, blend with its surroundings. I am awestruck at the wondrous colors of a vivid sunrise or sunset. These aspects of creation indeed speak of his glory. However, in humanity I am reminded of the beauty of his image. From the bright, alert eyes of a newborn infant to the cataract-clouded eyes of an elderly woman whose face is gracefully marked by the years of her journey, I am reminded that I am looking into eyes that resemble those of my Father.

In the most difficult parts of my life, when I begged to see the face of God, he gently taught (and continues to remind) me that I see his face in the face of those around me—the reassuring smile of my husband, the sparkling eyes of my daughter, the laughter-ridden, one-sided dimple of my son, and the proud gaze of my mother. They are the *poiema* of God, telling me of the depths of his love for me.

Digging Deeper into Creation, Creativity, & the Artist

As we move into our Bible study devotions, we will continue to explore the creation accounts of Genesis 1 and 2, as well as other passages that inform us about creation and our identity as children of and co-creators with God. Each study expounds on the ideas we have already examined as we go deeper into God's word. It is important that you have a copy of the Scriptures beside you as you study. You will want to begin by reading the passage in its entirety and understanding it in context with the Scriptures as a whole.

Whether you paint, sing, sculpt, act, mime, draw, design, carve, dance, or craft; whether you play an instrument, write poems or fiction or music or lyrics; whether you take photos, design websites, or create films—whatever your craft or art or performance, you are designed as God's workmanship, and he has a specific calling and purpose for your life. As you dig deeper into these scriptures, I pray:

that you will understand more fully your importance to the whole of creation;
that you will be affirmed in your role as an artist in this world and in the Church;
that you can embrace and enjoy your uniqueness as a creative type;
that you will understand your calling as God's child and *poiema*;
and that you will know the depths of God's love for you.

In God's glorious Name, amen.

Digging Deeper: Creation, Creativity, & the Artist

Genesis 1: Created for Covenant

Genesis 2: Containers of Clay

Psalm 19: The "Nature" of God

Psalm 139: Wonderfully Woven

Isaiah 43: Created, Formed, Redeemed, & Summoned

Digging Deeper:
Created for Covenant

Read: Genesis 1:26—2:3

We have already spent much time with this text and gleaned much from it:

- God is the source of creativity.
- We are made in his image. As his children, we resemble our Father.
- God says that we are *very* good and blesses us.
- We are God's workmanship—his *poiema*.

There is one more idea I want us to consider as we examine his word. While there are many more lessons that can be learned from this text, I want to focus on the covenantal relationship we have with our Father in heaven. In Genesis 1:1–25 we find God preparing the land for our habitation. Once we are placed there, he blesses us: "Be fruitful and increase in number; fill the earth and subdue it" (1:28). We see this covenant echoed throughout Scripture (i.e., Noah in Gen 9, Abraham in Gen 17, etc.). People and land are important to this covenant-making God, and this is established from the very beginning of our Bible.

The very phrase "in the beginning" is used by the authors of Scripture to mark a specific period of time, and it is implied to the reader that there is an "end" as well.[16] This clearly marks the beginning of history and denotes that there will also be an end. Within this context, God establishes a covenantal relationship with man and woman, the children he created. The importance of this blessing cannot be overlooked. It remains a central theme throughout Genesis and the Pentateuch.

God wants to bless his people. He didn't simply wind us up and let us go. He created us and desires an ongoing relationship with us. This is what it means to be in a covenantal relationship. When we marry, we enter a covenantal relationship. This is not someone who comes and goes out of our lives, but one committed to stay with us through the good and the bad. Our marriages are an earthly picture of a heavenly reality. God is in this for better or worse, and he has no intention of letting us go. *We* may not be faithful to the covenant, but that does not deter him. This is why we see the theme of adultery repeated over and over throughout Scripture. When we abandon our end of the covenant, we cheat on God. We find ourselves in the arms of another lover, and God is deeply saddened if not enraged.

Have you cheated on God?

Have you wandered off?

What things in your life pull you away from the covenantal relationship that God desires to have with you? How can you avoid those things? Can you pledge to be faithful to him?

What things can you do to bind yourself to this pledge?

This covenant?

This marriage with God?

Hosea 2:14–16 speaks of God's desire to bring us back into relationship with him: "Therefore I am now going to allure her; I will lead her into the desert and speak tenderly to her. There I will give her back her vineyards, and will make the Valley of Achor [meaning: trouble] a door of hope. There she will sing as in the days of her youth, as in the day she came up out of Egypt. 'In that day,' declares the LORD, 'you will call me 'my husband'; you will no longer call me 'my master.'" The book of Hosea is an excellent example of covenantal imagery and should be read in light of that truth.

God desires to bless you, your family, your ministry, your creative endeavors. However, this blessing is given within the context of this covenantal relationship. Like Adam and Eve, we find ourselves lured away by forbidden fruit and end up naked and ashamed. That isn't the relationship that God desires with you. He loves you. He will be faithful to you always and in all ways. Find blessing there in the safety of that loving relationship. Bind yourself to it. Renew your covenantal vows to him—right now, in this very moment. Let him make your Valley of Trouble a door of hope. Let him bless you with his love.

Listen to: "You Won't Relent" by Misty Edwards

Digging Deeper:
Containers of Clay

Read: Genesis 2:4–25

Where Genesis 1 finds us created "in the image of God," Genesis 2 finds us created "from the dust of the ground."[17] According to biblical scholar John Sailhamer, "In light of the special treatment given to man's creation in chapter 1, the emphasis in chapter 2 on man's 'creatureliness' is not without its importance."[18] We are reminded here that we are indeed earthly in nature, and that God has no problem with that! According to Peterson, "We are the identical stuff with the place in which we have been put. God formed us from dust, from dirt—the same stuff that we walk on every day." He continues, "Creation . . . is not something apart from us: it is part of us and we are a part of it."[19] This account places us squarely in the midst of creation, not as divine beings with equality to God, but humans created from this earth.

The image of potter and clay is evident here as God molds us from the material of this earth. We also see this image repeated by the prophets:

- You turn things upside down, as if the potter were thought to be like the clay! Shall what is formed say to the one who formed it, "You did not make me?" Can the pot say to the potter, "You know nothing?" (Isa 29:16)

- Yet you, LORD, are our Father. We are the clay, you are the potter; we are all the work of your hand. (Isa 64:8)

- "Can I not do with you, Israel, as this potter does?" declares the LORD. "Like clay in the hand of the potter, so are you in my hand, Israel." (Jer 18:6)

The writers of the Old Testament watch the potter create a vessel out of a formless mass of clay, and it becomes a powerful metaphor for God's creative action and power. In creation God becomes artist and creates a work of art from the raw materials he has created. And from that earthly raw material, our Creator brings us into being through the power of his life-giving breath.

Consider "breath" for a moment. Breath invades every cell of our body. Our body is lifeless without it. We need it to live. Likewise, breath needs something to contain it, to give it shape, to give it purpose. These things are true on a spiritual level, as well.

God invades every fiber of our being.
We are lifeless without him.
We need him to live.
And God needs someone to be his container.
To give him shape in this shapeless world.

Are you willing to be God's container? To give him shape? To be purposed by him to do his will and bring his Spirit to others? He still breathes into his people today. Before Christ ascended into heaven, he breathed on his disciples, telling them, "Receive the Holy Spirit" (John 20:22). The Holy Spirit is within and available to all who believe (Acts 2:38; Rom 5:5; 1 Cor 6:19; Eph 1:13–14; Titus 3:4–7). As an artist, let his life-giving breath fill and flow through you. Allow him to breath into the things that you create from the raw materials you've been given. Give him shape. Let him be purposed and give you purpose. Be his container.

Creator God, my Potter, mold me into your vessel. Breath of Life, fill me with more of your life-giving Spirit. Where I am broken, repair me; where I am unformed, mold me; where I am lifeless, breathe into me; where you need to be, let me be your vessel, your container, your life, your breath. In your life-giving Name, amen.

Listen to: "The Potter's Hand" by Darlene Zschech

Digging Deeper:
The "Nature" of God

Read: Psalm 19

As you read Psalm 19, you'll see it is broken into two parts: the first praises God as revealed through nature; and the second praises God as revealed in the Torah (his law). We see God speaking through both his creation and his word, and the psalmist is in wonder of them both. In the end, our biblical poet is brought to confession and prayer: "May the words of my mouth and the meditation of my heart be pleasing in your sight, O LORD, my Rock and my Redeemer" (v. 14).

For the artist, God often speaks through nature. Several years ago my husband, children, and I were driving along Interstate 70 in Colorado. The road cuts right through the mountains, and the drive between Vail and Glenwood Springs is incredible. On our left was the Eagle River—wide and winding, sparkling and beautiful—with the Denver/Rio Grand Western railway just beyond it. On our right were the mountains with their colorful striations. The whole drive was spectacular to me.

I kept pointing out sights as we drove: "Look kids! Look at how big that rock is!" And as we drove through a rock formation: "Kids, check this out—we're driving through a rock!"

"Yes, mother," came the patronizing tone of my children's voices from the back seat of the car. They were not nearly as amazed as I was.

I have always been awed by nature. I have learned many of God's truths through creation. When I witness something in nature I want everyone else to see and know the wonder-making, breath-taking, spirit-waking God of my soul. Biblical scholar Peter Craigie notes that the reflection of God in nature "is perceptible only to those already sensitive to God's revelation and purpose."[20] It pains me when others cannot see. How can you witness the awesome wonder of it all and not be changed? I am definitely a "stop-and-smell-the-roses" kind of gal! The beauty of creation was placed there for me to see and enjoy by the Maker of the Universe, and darn if I won't stop and take advantage of it!

One time my son and I were listening to "Open the Eyes of My Heart" by singer and worship leader Paul Baloche on the radio in the car. The last lines of the song rang out just before we got out of the car to run our errand. He asked me a question that tore at my heart: "Mom, can we really *see* God?" I was in one of those seasons of my life when God was both silent and unseen. As I paused to gather myself, I prayed: "Good question, God. Now, how do I answer my child when *I'm* not even sure you exist sometimes?"

From somewhere beyond me the answer spilled from my lips, "Well, Evan, we see God all around us—in nature, in people . . ."

Quick on the wonderment of it all, he piped in, "Yeah, Mom! You're right! Look! We can see him here in this flower and in this spider-ant!" The flower was a dandelion weed and the "spider-ant" was really just a creepy spider. But even in the things of creation that some would find troublesome or annoying, my son saw God.

> "Yeah, buddy, and I see God in you," came my shaky voice as I choked back tears. Out of the mouths of babes.

> *Can we look at both the rose and the dandelion and see God?*
> *Can we admire a regal praying mantis or a "spider-ant" and see God's hand in both?*
> *Can we see God in those we love and in those "extra grace required" people in our lives?*

Lord, grant us eyes to see and ears to hear. When it seems you are far off and nowhere to be found, reveal yourself to us in new ways. Open our hearts, minds, and spirits to you. Reveal yourself to us in not just the holy, sacred things, but in the simple things, as well. And do not let creation cry out while we are silent. Let us sing of the beauty of your majesty, grace, and love. May the words of our mouths and the meditations of our hearts be pleasing in your sight, O Lord, our Rock and our Redeemer. Amen.

Listen to: "Open the Eyes of My Heart" by Paul Baloche

Digging Deeper:
Wonderfully Woven

Read: Psalm 139

Psalm 139 is one of my favorite passages of Scripture. It tells of his protective love and covering over us. It reminds us that no matter where we are in life, no matter how far we've gone astray, no matter what problems assail us, he is there, and he knows what we're going through. In the midst of this, we find these verses that again hearken back to the creation narratives. Instead of the potter/clay image, we find another artistic image: that of a textile weaver. This image is also used in Job 10:8–12 as we see God knitting together skin, flesh, bones, and sinew—God as the Master Weaver.

Have you ever examined the back of a tapestry? It is a mess! All the threads cross over one another and stick out in disarray. However, when you turn it over, its true image is revealed, and you can see how all the threads come together to create something cohesive and beautiful. Our lives are like a tapestry.

The Master Weaver takes all these threads and pieces and entwines them together.

It takes time.

It's a slow process.

Seems as if it may never be complete.

Sometimes we look at our lives from the back and we hardly understand. It seems there's no pattern, no rhyme nor reason, to the threads and their pattern. Pieces stick out. There are knots. The edges are frayed. There are places where dark threads seem to be matted together, thick and muddled. There are places of vibrant color, but even the color seems in disarray.

Nothing makes sense.

However, at the end of our lives, the Master Weaver will turn us over, and a magnificent tapestry will be revealed. Can we wait? Can we trust that what seems like chaos is actually an intricately woven pattern of beauty?

Hannah was a blonde, curly-headed girl with Down's Syndrome from our first church in Columbus, Ohio. Her shy smile and giggle were infectious. When she was still quite young, she died in a tragic accident at her home. In many respects, the tapestry of her life still does not make sense. At least to us. But the Master Weaver, who had ordained all the days of her precious life, has already turned over her tapestry to reveal its beauty to all the angels and saints gathered there at her homecoming. And as she plays at the foot of the magnificent throne of heaven, God watches over her and smiles at the beauty of his work.

As we examine the fabric of our lives, dear Lord, may we be mindful of your hand gently weaving and creating a tapestry of beauty. Grant us patience in the process. Help us to trust the places that don't make sense. In the end, may you turn us over to reveal your glory—woven there through the weft and warp of our lives. We praise you, Lord, for we know that we are fearfully and wonderfully made. By the Weaver's hand, amen.

Listen to: "Fearfully, Wonderfully Made" by Matt Redman

Digging Deeper:
Created, Formed, Redeemed, & Summoned

Read: Isaiah 43:1-7

Consider these words from Isaiah 43:

Created — Hebrew: *bara* – to create, to bring about, do. Indicates a new creative act rather than a refashioning of an object after its original creation. Signifies bringing into existence.

Formed — Hebrew: *yasar* – to form, fashion, devise, produce, create; to be formed or fashioned. The word implies initiation as well as structuring. *Yasar* is often used of God's creative acts and denotes a potter or creator.

Redeemed — Hebrew: *gaal* – to redeem, ransom, release, deliver; to fulfill the duties of relationship. The main idea is that of buying back something or someone, something consecrated to God.

Summoned — Hebrew: *qara* – to cry out, call; to name; to proclaim, pronounce, preach. Essentially denotes the enunciation of a specific message, usually addressed to a specific recipient, and intended to elicit a specific response.

It is amazing what the original language of a Scripture passage reveals. Soak in the definitions above and read the passage in light of the depth of meaning we see here. *Created* is the same essence as what we have found in Genesis 1. Note here the idea of *creatio ex hililo*, which we saw in Tillich's ideas on creation. *Formed* is the same essence as Genesis 2 and echoes the potter/clay image. Note the relational aspect found in the definition of *redeemed*—reminding us of God's covenantal relationship with us his consecrated people (Genesis 1) and the lengths to which he will go to bring us back. And then we find the word *summoned*.

> The Lord God, your Creator, has cried out for you,
>   calling you *specifically by name*
>   with a specific message
>   and for a specific purpose.
>   He has proclaimed that you are his!

And no matter what happens in your life, the situations that surround you, the circumstances that you find yourself in—God is there protecting you. This is a remarkable passage that speaks (perhaps screams) of God's desire for the love of his life—you!

Think of how sometimes as an artist it is so difficult to step back from your work and critically analyze it or, heaven forbid, have someone else critique it. We become attached to our creative visions and often have a hard time making adjustments to our work. As an artist, however, we know that this is necessary to create with excellence and integrity. But God is the Artist above all artists.

Genesis 1 reveals a God who does indeed step back to inspect his work, yet each time he does so, he still proclaims, "It is good." There is no need to make adjustments because he got it right each time. And God is very attached to his work. He loves it, and he loves how it turned out. And this attachment to his work is revealed in his unrelenting love for his people. Each time his people fail to live up to the covenants he has established with them, he still takes them back. Yes, there is rebuke and correction, but God is so attached to his creative work that he takes them back, sets them straight, and stands back to admire once again.

When he created you, he had a specific purpose in mind. As you align yourself to God's good and perfect will, his purposes are made clear. As you walk in his ways and plans for your life, he steps back and admires his work. Listen. He is calling you—by name:

"_____, You are mine!"

(Your name above)

Listen to: "Remedy" by Aaron Wardle

Endnotes

1. Kegley, *Paul Tillich*, 4–10. All Paul Tillich research and information is taken from this source.

2. Kuyper, *Calvinism*, as quoted in Begbie, *Voicing Creation's Praise*, 98.

3. Begbie, *Voicing Creation's Praise*, 156.

4. Kelly, *Testament*, 33, 73–74.

5. Begbie, *Voicing Creation's Praise*, 177.

6. Ibid.

7. As quoted in ibid., 206.

8. Foster, *Streams*, 260.

9. Begbie, *Voicing Creation's Praise*, 206.

10. Ibid., 257. Note Begbie's tie to community in this statement.

11. I am not using the term "co-creators" as an indication that we are on par or equal to God in the creation process, but to indicate how we work alongside, in cooperation with, and in subjection to God as the first and foremost Divine Creator.

12. Begbie, *Voicing Creation's Praise*, 179–80.

13. Hart, "Through the Arts," 18.

14. Gunkel, *Genesis*, 112.

15. Peterson, *Christ Plays*, 53.

16. Sailhamer, "Genesis," 20.

17. The Hebrew for man (*adam*) sounds like and may be related to the Hebrew for ground (*adamah*). It is also the name Adam (see Gen 2:20).

18. Sailhamer, "Genesis," 41.

19. Peterson, *Christ Plays*, 76.

20. Craigie, *Psalms 1–50*, 181.

two

Incarnational Ministry:
Being the Hands & Feet of Christ

"In the beginning was the Word . . .
. . . and the Word became flesh and dwelled among us."

ONCE AGAIN: "IN THE beginning . . ." It is no accident that the writer of the Gospel of John repeats the introductory words of the Hebrew Bible, for in John we find the creation story re-created through the story of redemption. The original "In the beginning" story is one that has been part of the oral tradition of the nation of Israel long before it was ever written down. It is a story that is many thousands of years old. And in these opening words of John, we find the beginning of a new creation story. There is a new Adam—an Adam who existed from before time, who was part of the creation of the universe—the Word—Christ, God Incarnate.

> After a long history of failure and faithfulness, persecution and promise, the people of God are given a fresh start. These phrases [found in John 1] echo the words of Genesis. This new beginning is redolent of God's great beginning acts, and its purpose is to restore the original shape and intention to creation. But this beginning is more than earth and sky, element and creature, it is the beginning of wisdom and understanding. "In the beginning was the Word." A Word beyond etymology and philology, this Word is the life and light of humanity. This Word has the power to make us new creatures and to give us new life.[1]

John is deliberately starting his gospel with these words to connect it to the original Genesis story and his intention is to identify Christ with the

Word that existed before creation. And according to Peterson, "The same Word that brought creation into being is Jesus, who now brings a new creation into being."[2]

Incarnation—Big Word, Big Idea

The doctrine of the Incarnation is fundamental to Christianity. Karl Barth puts forth that the Incarnation is central to our Christian faith in that all other theology needs to be addressed in light of the fact that God "became flesh and made his dwelling among us" (John 1:14).[3] In its literal terms, "incarnation" means "enfleshment" or "embodiment in flesh" or "clothe with flesh." The concept of the Incarnation developed in the first several centuries of the Christian church to help understand and give theological meaning to the phrase *sarx egeneto* found in John 1:14, which is typically translated "became flesh."[4] According to New Testament scholar James Dunn, the idea of incarnation could be used for "any embodiment in any flesh," and could also be applied to all believers as sons and daughters of God (Acts 17:28, Gal 4:4–7).[5] For this reason, I will refer to the Christ event (birth, life, death, resurrection) as the Incarnation (capital I)[6] and the idea of God or Christ in humanity as incarnation (small i).

According to Ross Langmead, "The very idea of Incarnation involves an implied contrast between divinity and humanity, a striking difference which is overcome by God."[7] And Marianne Thompson tells us, "The 'Word became flesh' means that the Creator entered the sphere of createdness."[8] What both Langmead and Thompson are getting at here is key to our Christian understanding of the Incarnation: Christ was both and at the same time fully God/divine and fully man/human. While this belief is central to the doctrine, it was not without much thought and debate, especially throughout early church history. Peterson affirms the fully God/fully man tenet: "In Jesus Christ we see the Creator at work among us (very God); in him we also see the creation of which we are a part (very Man)."[9] The Bible holds this paradox in tightly balanced tension, and according to Hart, for the artist in particular: "Both poles of the tension are important to hold on to."[10]

It is with this most basic understanding of the doctrine of the Incarnation that we move forward. At this point, you might be asking what all this theological talk has to do with the artist. Must we be bothered with all of this? I believe that an incarnational understanding is critical to the artist for several reasons. As believers we must understand that, as "fully human," Christ experienced what we experience, yet as "fully God," Christ was able to live a life of power within the context of a sacrificial ministry. Through this Incarnation, he redeemed both humanity and creation. As artists, we can live spiritually abundant lives (John 10:10) within a world created by God for us without any degradation of the creation from which we derive the raw material we use to create. For the dancing "artist" whose medium is his or her body, a proper understanding of the redemption of our bodies is crucial. Therefore, I will spend some time addressing that area of artistry in particular. Finally, in this redemption, we bear the image of God in Christ and become his hands and feet. In this context, we will discuss the way of an incarnational life, faith, and ministry.

Fully Man—Christ's Humanity

First, let us look at Christ's humanity. When we explore this concept of Christ as fully man, we come to realize that he understands us as earth-bound human forms. Whether we experience great joy or deep pain, we know that Christ also experienced a full range of emotions. The Gospel of John makes deliberate effort to demonstrate Christ's humanness: he was tired and thirsty (4:6–7; 19:28); he was troubled, moved to compassion and shed tears for his friends (11:33–35); he suffered great anguish (12:27); he was hurt by betrayal (13:21); and he cared for his family (19:26).[11] We also see many examples of Christ's humanity throughout the book of Hebrews. In chapter 2, for example, we see that Christ is not only our family (v. 17), but also:

- he suffered death (v. 9);
- he was perfected through suffering (v. 10);
- he shared in our humanity (v. 14);
- he was made like his brothers and sisters in every way (v. 17);
- he suffered and was tempted (v. 18).

Because of this, Christ has become our Great High Priest and is able to sympathize with us in all situations (4:15). Although he was tempted, as we are, he did not fall into sin, and because of his strength and obedience we can boldly approach God's beautiful throne of mercy and grace (4:16).

There are many more scriptures pointing to Christ's humanity found in the New Testament, as well.

As artists, it is not just God's Spirit creating in and through us, but it is very much our own spirit embodied within us. From the depths of our experiences—from our pain, loss, and disappointment; from our laughter, joy, and happiness—we draw like water from a well. That water spills onto and into the works we create. Do not take this lightly or flippantly: God is using that well of experience to help you be a better artist, musician, dancer, actor, craftsman, filmmaker, and designer. More importantly, Christ is there in all of it, helping you draw more and more deeply from the well of your human experience.

Psychologist and former professional dancer Sara Savage pushes us to see that our humanity is very much a part of who we are as creators. She states:

> Although it is easier to divorce ourselves from the messiness of embodied human life, its emotional anguish and physical pains, and to prefer a 'spiritualized' Christianity, in doing so, we lose sight of much of the human reality of Christ's earthly life. Through the nourishment of the physical and emotional aspects of our experience, we come to a deeper person knowledge of ourselves, and, amidst a degree of unknowing, of Christ, who shares our humanity even though he is not still physically present to us in bodily form.[12]

Christ—our God, Incarnated into the same matter from which we ourselves were fashioned—shares our humanity. He is our brother—a brother that both participates in (fully man) and saves us from (fully God) the difficulties of our humanity.

Fully God—Christ's Divinity

Next, our incarnational approach also encompasses Christ's divinity. While the books of John and Hebrews attest to Christ's humanity, they also point to his divinity. Throughout John, we see Christ referring to himself with many "I am" statements:

- *I am* the bread of life (6:35ff).
- *I am* the light of the world (8:12; 9:5).
- *I am* from above (8:23).

- *I am* the gate (10:7, 9).

- *I am* the good shepherd (10:11, 14).

- *I am* the resurrection and the life (11:25).

- *I am* the way and the truth and the life (14:6).

- *I am* the true vine (15:1, 5).

And most unflinchingly: "I tell you the truth, before Abraham was born, *I AM!*" (8:58). This "I AM" phrase is connected to God's words to Moses: "I am who I am. This is what you are to say to the Israelites: 'I AM has sent me to you'" (Exod 3:14). This linked Christ directly and divinely to God. The book of Hebrews also is filled with many references to Christ's divinity. It begins with a beautiful hymn ascribing glory and honor to the risen Christ. Throughout the book of Hebrews, the author first establishes that Christ is higher than the angels (1:4–14), then greater than Moses (3:1–6), and finally, firmly establishes Christ as the Great High Priest (4:14—5:10, 7:11ff). The New Testament is filled with many more examples.

It is through Christ's God-nature that we find his power to redeem creation. We know that if Christ had come only as a man, he would not have had the power to overcome death on the cross and rise again from the tomb. His divinity and connection to God the Father gave him authority and dominion over sin, death, and hell. And it is through this death and resurrection that we have our redemption as sons and daughters of God. The Apostle Paul writes in Romans that we have been "set free" because God sent "his own Son in the likeness of sinful man to be a sin offering," therefore, "condemning sin in sinful man" (8:2–3). While Christ's *humanity* ties him to creation, and Christ's *divinity* allows for the redemption of creation, it is through his *humanity and divinity combined* that we are re-created!

A New Creation

Through God's Word Incarnated, a new creation is brought about through a new Adam. We live under a new covenant established through this new Adam, Jesus Christ. "Behold, I make all things new," proclaims the gospel of Jesus Christ (Rev 21:5, NKJV). We are indeed a "new creation" (2 Cor 5:17) in him. According to Hart, there is great artistry in this: "He takes our 'flesh', together with all its limiting factors and inherent flaws, and through a work of supremely 'inspired' (Spirit-filled) artistry, transfigures it, before handing it back to us in the glorious state which its original maker always intended it to bear. At this level creation, redemption, and re-creation are shown to be interwoven as activities of the same divine Poet."[13] Langmead also speaks to this re-creation:

> This perspective closely links creation and redemption, just as the Prologue to John's Gospel [John 1] does when it identifies the divine creative Word with Jesus Christ the Word who "became flesh and lived among us" (John 1:14). It takes the structure of the Incarnation (which is the embodiment and enfleshment) and reads it back into the heart of God. Our human experience of God, then, can be interpreted as "incarnation," the transformation of the present by the creative and powerful force which is God creating and re-creating humanity through the mystery of Christ.[14]

And Jesus commands us to help him in the redemption of creation: "Go into all the world and preach the good news to all creation" (Mark 16:15). The gospel (good news) is that we have been redeemed, and it is our life's vocation to proclaim this to all of creation. As artists, one of the many ways we do this is through our creative work. Our redemption and freedom through Christ has a vital role in this. Begbie speaks to this:

> In Christ, the incarnate Son, through the operation of the Spirit, our self-centered humanity has been made responsive—to the Father, to others, and to our created environment. It has been freed—which is to say it has been enabled to relate and respond appropriately to reality. In Christ, our personhood has been reconstituted in its true relatedness. It is the work of the Spirit in us to bring about (albeit provisionally) what he has already accomplished in the Son. In the artist, by extension, the Spirit will make possible that free, purposeful interaction with the Creator, with one another and the world around us.[15]

We must understand that through Jesus Christ we are redeemed creators given redeemed creation with materials and mediums with which to work. The Holy Spirit guides us in our interaction with this creation in order to interpret it for those around us. Our religious culture can sometimes view our material world as suspect. Through Christ we are called to reclaim it, affirm it, complete it, and transform it—not overturn it, condemn it, or degrade it.[16] In Genesis we saw that creation was proclaimed "very good." As new creations, we affirm again its goodness and reveal the good news through this goodness.

Our Bodies Redeemed

At this point, I want to speak specifically to those who use their bodies as their artistic medium—those in dance, mime, creative movement, drama, acrobatics, or any other artistic form that uses the body. Two thousand years ago, Plato taught about the higher nature of the spirit and the lower nature of the flesh.[17] Interestingly, this went directly against the more holistic mindset of the Hebrew people, who considered the person as a whole being—mind, body, spirit, soul—and not as fragmented and fractured pieces.[18] Add to that the Enlightenment period, which placed the mind and knowledge above the heart and feelings, and we have a dangerous mix that denigrates anything physical or felt.

We have long fought the mindset that as artists who use our bodies we are somehow less than others. And in some extreme cases throughout church history, we have been downright banned from expressing our worship through dance in any way. In some churches, that ban still stands today. It is sad to think that we must check our bodies at the door, like coats in a coat check, as if they are something cumbersome to be set aside so that we can be truly holy.

Genesis 1 and 2 declare that we are very good, created in his image, and God's beautiful artistic sculpture. Note that before the fall, our bodies were naked, and we were unashamed. In the fall, we became self-conscious of our physical body and began to cover it up so that God and others could not see (as if with leaves, animal skins, or clothing we could cover our true nature). In God's original plan, our bodies were a beautiful part of the creation story. Then, amazingly, Christ came to redeem creation through the medium of flesh—a *physical human body*!

How can we continue to condemn that which God has declared "very good"? That which Christ took on in earthly form? That which Christ redeemed through his death and resurrection? And that which the Holy Spirit indwells as his temple? In Christ, our bodies are redeemed—both here on earth and in a future sense, in heaven. We have already discussed how Christ's atoning work redeemed (past atoning tense) and will redeem (future heavenly tense) all of creation, including our bodies (see 1 Cor 15; Rev 20–21), even if it is in a manner that we cannot comprehend. This redemption is true of our entire being—heart, soul, mind, *and* body.

In an article entitled "Embodying Praise," Jeannette Batz interviewed theologian Karen Armstrong, who had once served as a nun in the Catholic Church. Armstrong shared these thoughts: "Christians should have valued the body more than any other faith, because we believe God valued it so much he took it himself. But it didn't work out that way, and that's a tragedy."[19] Ironically, C.S. Lewis (writing some fifty years earlier) stated the complete opposite. According to Lewis, "Christianity is almost the only one of the great religions which thoroughly approves of the body—which believes that matter is good, that God himself once took on a human body, that some kind of body is going to be given us even in Heaven and is going to be an essential part of our happiness, our beauty, and our energy."[20] Can it be that we have actually regressed in our thoughts about the human body? Or is there a dichotomy in our thought? While some denominations have fully embraced the use of dance and movement in their worship, others have banned it.

I am part of a denomination that has traditionally condemned dancing, but I have seen a definite shift in my lifetime. In fact, the ministry I oversee has danced at many annual denominational conferences. I believe that where there has been abuse the "baby has been thrown out with the bath water," so to speak. Instead, we must address the true problems. We must help ministry leaders understand the holiness with which we must approach the body and its related art forms in worship. It is indeed a tragedy that churches would take what God and Christ have affirmed and condemn it as if we are all still fallen creatures, unworthy of redemption. It is an even greater tragedy if that has happened at the hands of the artists themselves due to poor judgment and less than sound doctrinal understanding of this beautiful ministry.

Incarnational Ministry

Now finally, let us return to the subject of Christ's Incarnation and what that means for the artist in terms of an incarnational ministry, faith, and life. As Christian artists, we are called to an incarnational life that imitates the Incarnated Christ. Richard Foster includes a whole chapter on what it means to live an incarnational life in his book *Streams of Living Water*. In summary, Foster states that the incarnational life "focuses upon making present and visible the realm of the invisible spirit. This sacramental way of living addresses the crying need to experience God as truly manifest and notoriously active in daily life."[21]

What does this mean? Simply, Christ lived and walked here on planet earth. However, Christ is no longer here in flesh. In his risen state, he is here in spirit through the power of the Holy Spirit living in and working through our lives. In an incarnational life, we become the embodiment of Christ—we become his hands and feet—through the power of the Holy Spirit.

The New Testament lays out for us a pattern of living in the person of Jesus Christ. We are to be his hands as we serve. We are called to be his feet as we spread the good news of his saving grace to those with whom we come in contact. This is more than just asking ourselves, "What would Jesus do?" and doing what it is we think he'd do. It is asking ourselves, "What would Jesus see, hear, think, feel, and how then would he react in response to those sights, sounds, thoughts, and emotions?"

We need to see others with his eyes and hear what others are saying as if Jesus himself were sitting there with us. We need to filter our own thoughts and preferences through Christ's mind. We need to feel compassion as Jesus did. Throughout the Gospels, we see Christ moved to compassion by the people around him (Matt 9:36; 14:14; 15:32; 20:34; Mark 1:41; 6:34; 8:2; Luke 15:20). He didn't come just to die, but to live a life of ministry to the people. We often focus so much on the sacrifice of Christ's *atoning* work that we forget the sacrifice of his *ministerial* work.

In very practical ways, this might mean many things to us as artistic co-creators. We could volunteer our time at an inner-city school without the funds to hire an art or music teacher. We could paint a large mural displaying God's glory on an unsightly building. We could give a broke college student free music lessons. We could speak or perform free of charge. We could produce a film at cost for an organization that serves the poor. We could offer hip-hop or step classes at a church in an underserved area of town. We could find another creative person who could otherwise not afford music, art, dance, or acting lessons, and pour into them.

You get the point. I'm not simply talking about volunteerism. I'm talking about giving something of worth to people, offering others hope, and making God's glory real in their lives through creativity and art. I'm talking about giving something of ourselves in a sacrificial way that embodies Christ to those who do not know him. This is the incarnational life of faith, service, and love.

We are called to make real Christ's presence here on earth to people who "need to see it to believe it." Art by its very nature is highly symbolic. Through our art we make the invisible visible, we make the inaudible audible. As artists, we have the opportunity to help others see what cannot be seen and hear what cannot be heard. Begbie implores us: "There should be no withdrawal into the refuge of a religious ghetto, but instead a longing to spread the aroma of Christ into every corner of culture, not least the arts."[22]

Do the things you do as an artist spread his aroma or simply smell of your own self-pride and promotion? We must realize that we serve as the hands and feet of Christ in a world that longs to see, feel, touch, and know that God is indeed real and not some spiritual crutch. Like Christ, we must speak words that bring life, freedom, and healing to those around us. Through the power of the Holy Spirit, we are the incarnation of Christ. I summarize this section with the words of a very wise artist, Father Robert VerEecke. Ponder them a moment before you move on: "My own journey as an artist in the Church has been a continual attempt to believe and affirm in myself the truth of the incarnation; that in yearning to express the deepest core of human life through gestures, the movement, the dances I make, I am in touch with and bring to expression the mystery of God's creative and incarnate life."[23]

Digging Deeper into Incarnational Ministry

With these thoughts in mind, we move into our Bible studies. Again, you will want to have a copy of the Scriptures by your side as we examine these passages. You will notice as we progress through them that we will remain with this theme of the Incarnation and incarnation, as we start at his birth in Matthew and end with his final restoration of all creation in Revelation. These scriptures reveal both the divine and human nature of Christ. They also encourage us to accept the gift that is freely offered in the person of Christ. We will also explore the dual ideas of imitating Christ and being conformed to his image.

I pray that as you delve deeper into Scripture:
God will continue to reveal his Word made flesh to you;
the Incarnation will be made real to you through the person of Christ;
you will understand and worship Christ more fully as you read of him;
you will know your importance as the hands and feet of our
Beautiful Risen Lord, Jesus Christ, Messiah, Savior, Friend.

In Christ's most precious Name, amen.

Digging Deeper: Incarnational Ministry

Matthew 1: What's in a Name?

Hebrews 1: Reflecting Christ's Radiance

Colossians 1: Holy, Without Blemish and Free

Philippians 2: Conformed to His Image

Revelation 21: All Things New

Digging Deeper:
What's in a Name?

Read: Matthew 1:1-25

Here we find Matthew's account of the birth of Christ. From the very first verse, Matthew takes great pains to establish Christ's identity as rightful Messiah, true Son of God, and ruling king over all Israel. Verse one links his lineage to two people: King David, ruler of the throne from which the Messiah will descend, and Abraham, the father of the nation of Israel. As we continue this story of origins, Matthew also makes it clear that this child is a new creation through the power of the Holy Spirit (fully God). Yet, he is born of an earthly woman (fully man). This deliberately echoes the Spirit of God breathing into the nostrils of the man made from clay in the beginning of creation (Gen 2:7).[24] Matthew then connects this miraculous birth to the prophecy of Isaiah that foretold of a virgin birth as a sign from the Lord (7:14).

It is important to note the meaning of names to the Hebrew people. When children were born, names were chosen carefully and often became a self-fulfilling prophecy over the child's life. When my children were born we gave them names that we liked, and it wasn't until later that we realized the beautiful meanings of their names. Madelyn Ruth (after my paternal grandmother) means "Magnificent Companion" and Evan Godfrey (after my husband's father) means "Young Warrior for God's Peace."

What is most interesting is that their characters and personalities are much like their given name meanings. Madelyn is a friend to all. One of her teachers once said, "Everyone thinks they are Madelyn's best friend." She has a way of making her friends feel valued. Our son, Evan is very kind and compassionate. He once was given the honor of being selected as a "peace patrol" at his school because of his ability to help others work out their differences. He spreads God's peace wherever he goes. God knew them before they were born, and the Holy Spirit was obviously involved in our selection of their names. My nightly prayer for them is that they will walk boldly in their meanings.

It is almost ridiculous to say that God knew Christ before he was born. But it is important to realize that God had a specific purpose for Jesus and that is reflected in his name. Jesus knew that purpose and walked boldly in obedience in order to fulfill what he came to do. Matthew tells us that

Immanuel means "God with Us," which tells us that Jesus came to be God among his people—God, as Christ, walking among his children—teaching them, touching them, healing them, feeding them, restoring them.

The name Jesus is a Greek form of the Hebrew name Joshua, which means "The Lord Saves," which speaks of Christ as Savior. Like a mighty warrior, God comes through his Son as the Messiah who would save his people. When Christ was handed the scroll to read in the synagogue, this is what he read: "The Spirit of the Lord is on me, because he has anointed me to preach good news to the poor. He has sent me to proclaim freedom for the prisoners and recovery of sight for the blind, to release the oppressed, to proclaim the year of the Lord's favor" (Luke 4:18–19). This, of course, is a direct reference to the words of the prophet Isaiah found in 61:1–2. What a wonderful picture of Christ knowing his purpose, declaring it, and walking in it.

Do you know your purpose?

What does your name mean? Is it prophetic in any way?

Even the titles given to you...

artist ...   photographer ...   painter ...
musician ...   singer ...   filmmaker ...   writer ...
poet ...   designer ...   dancer ...

What does that mean? And how does that define your purpose?

What about these names?

Child of God ...   Beloved ...   Bride of Christ ...
Radiant ...   Daughter of Zion ...   Sons of God ...
Chosen of God ...   His *Poiema* ...   Conquerors ...

Consider what *that* means? How does *that* define your purpose?

I have a piece of Mary Anne Radmacher's poetic art[25] with a beautiful paraphrase of Jeremiah 31:3–4 sitting in my kitchen where I can see it.

It tells me, reminds me, that I am "Loved by God."

Pray specifically about your name this week. Look up the meaning of your name. Is there something prophetic there? Ask God to help you uncover the name he gave you before you were even born. Perhaps it's not your given name. Perhaps it's another.

Ask him to reveal the name and its meaning.
How can you be defined by God's name for you
and the purpose wrapped up in that?
Can you walk boldly in that name?
I pray that you can and do. Amen.

Listen to: "Rolling Thunder" by Mandy Joy Miller

Digging Deeper:
Reflecting Christ's Radiance

Read: Hebrews 1:1–4

This short intro to the book of Hebrews reflects some of the same thoughts as those found in John 1. For example, we have Christ as the spoken Word of God. He is the same Word that brought the universe into being. The Son's radiance is like the "true light" (John 1:9) and God's glory is like the "glory of the One and Only" (John 1:14). However, there is one very big difference.

In John 1, the world does not recognize Christ, and humankind rejects him. However, in Hebrews 1 Christ is recognized as the Savior of the world, seated at the right hand of God, and elevated above the angels. After taking the rest of the chapter to establish Christ superiority over God's angels, the writer then says: "We must pay more careful attention, therefore, to what we have heard, so that we do not drift away" (2:1). He then emphatically states that we cannot ignore the message of salvation that was given to us through Christ and made evident through signs, wonders, and miracles, as well as the outpouring of the Holy Spirit.

It is important that we pay careful attention to the message of God through the Word, Jesus Christ. How often do we let distractions, doubt, or regret drown out the Word of God in our own lives? Does the volume of this world threaten to overpower the still small voice that speaks in the quiet of our hearts? I must confess that I can get awfully distracted with the pace of life going at full speed around me. It is easy to get caught in the tailspin of it all. It is vital that I spend time in the Lord's presence each day; that I pay "careful attention" to God speaking in my life.

When Moses came down from Mt. Sinai after spending time in God's presence, his face was so radiant that the people couldn't look at him, and he had to wear a veil over his face to address the people (Exod 34). Psalm 34:5 also tells us: "Those who look to him are radiant: their faces are never covered with shame." There is something about spending time in the Lord's presence that gives radiance to our countenance.

Several years ago, I had to have surgery to remove a cyst on my vocal cord. Following the surgery, I wasn't allowed to speak at all for three days. So, I dedicated those three days to reflection and prayer through solitude and silence. The second day, I was very tired and spent the entire day drifting in and out of sleep. Each time I awoke, I would pray and worship God through silence until I drifted off again. The next day, I had enough energy to read my Bible as well. During those days, God's presence with me was so real it was nearly palpable—like a comforting blanket, it enveloped me in peace. A couple days later I went to our church staff prayer meeting (even though I was only allowed to speak a few words each hour). As I walked in, our youth pastor asked how I was doing. All I could do was smile and nod my head.

He laughed as he said, "It's as if God's presence is radiating all around you."

I could surely feel it, and it was apparently visible to others. As we spend time communing with him and meditating on his word, our lives begin to reflect the glory of God. On the other hand, when we fail to spend time with God, our lives and our very countenance become dull and lack luster.

Read the passage from Hebrews again and listen to God speaking through his Son. These four short verses speak volumes of Christ's worthiness and splendor.

> By the power of his word, he sustains all of creation.
> He is the exact representation of God's glorious being.
> He is seated at the right hand of God in heaven.
> He provides purification for our sins.

When we make Christ the center of our lives, we reflect his glory in our lives. There is no better way to be the hands and feet of Christ than to be with Christ each day. Picture him walking with you as you go to the store. Imagine him next to you as you sit through your next business meeting. As you hold the hand of a friend in comfort, envision him holding the other hand. When you pray for someone, think of him there on the other side of them praying right along with you. If you want your hands-and-feet incarnational life to reflect the radiant glory of Christ, you must pay attention to him. Read stories from the four Gospel accounts, picturing yourself there with Christ, watching him, learning from him, ministering with him. Allow him to teach you through your encounters with his Word.

Let your artwork reflect his glory, too. As you soak in his glorious presence, it will spill over into that which you create. You are his hands and feet. You reflect his glory through your life, ministry, artwork, and creativity. As you work through the creative process, ask him to be there with you, guiding you. Check in with him as you create. Step back and ask, "So, Jesus, what do you think? Does this reflect you? How can I reflect you better?" and listen to his response. Let him be your instructor, your tutor, your mentor as you learn to create pieces that reflect his glory. In this way, even the "non-religious" pieces you create will speak of his presence in your life. Let him be reflected in you, through you.

May God's face shine down on you;
> may his light shine through you;
>> and may God be reflected in you and all that you do.
>>> In his glorious Name, amen.

Listen to: "Great I Am" by New Life Worship

Digging Deeper:
Holy, Without Blemish and Free

Read: Colossians 1:15–23

What a beautiful passage this is! It paints this amazing picture of Christ and then surprisingly paints us into that same picture! The first part is said to be a hymn of the early Christian church. Again, this passage reflects the same thoughts and images found in both Genesis 1 and John 1, and Paul is purposely drawing a connection from Christ back to the Old Testament creation story in this passage.[26] The word for "image" found in verse 15 is the Greek word *eikon*. This word "always assumes a prototype (the original form from which the image is drawn), not merely a thing it resembles."[27] With God as the ultimate prototype, Christ is an exact representation. He doesn't just share a resemblance to God—he *is* the image of God, based on a perfect prototype.

It is through God's representation on earth that we who were alienated are now reconciled to God through the death of his Son's physical body. Jesus became the final sacrificial lamb. And we are not only *saved* by his death, but we are *presented holy in God's sight.* Paul is clear: we must hold fast to the good news we have been given. This isn't just "fire insurance." This is the good news of Jesus Christ sacrificed and now risen for us all!

The Incarnational message of Christ in this passage is obvious:
Image of the invisible God;
    Firstborn over all creation;
        All things created through and for him;
            Before all things;
                Sustainer of all things;
                    Head of the body, the church;
                        The beginning;
                          Risen supreme!
The fullness of God dwells in him;
    All things are reconciled through him;
        He makes peace through his blood, shed on the cross for you and me!
            Through that reconciliation, we are presented
                holy, without blemish, and *free* from accusation.

I am filled with both remorse and loving amazement at the thought of my Savior dying on a cross for me. My eyes often well up with tears at the wonder of it! The perfect Sacrificial Lamb dying in my place, for my own shortcomings, for my own failures, for my own selfish pride. Ponder these words from the hymn "When I Survey the Wondrous Cross" written by Isaac Watts in 1707:

> See from His head, His hands, His feet,
> Sorrow and love flow mingled down;
> Did e'r such love and sorrow meet,
> Or thorns compose so rich a crown?

How brilliantly he depicts the blood of Christ as a beautiful mixture of sorrow and love. How sweetly he describes the majestic crown of thorns.

It brings us face to face with the magnificent atrocity and scandalous beauty of the passion of Christ.

> *I was once a child alienated from my Father in heaven.*
> *Now, I am brought before him—*
> *presented to him—*
> *as holy, without blemish and free*
> *through the body and blood of Christ.*

Say those words out loud—not as me writing them, but *you* saying them, affirming them as God's honest truth! Are you in wonder? Are you mournful? Are you elated? Do you marvel at this wondrous cross and what it means to you? Spend some time today meditating on the sacrifice that Christ, the firstborn of all creation, made on your behalf, in your place. Your praise and adoration of him is all he desires in return for the beautiful gift he gives.

> *Listen to: "When I Survey the Wondrous Cross"*
> *by one of your favorite artists*

Digging Deeper:
Conformed to His Image

Read: Philippians 2:1–18

This early writing of Paul appears to be either a hymn or creedal statement. At first glance, it may appear that in making himself nothing (emptying himself), Christ was not fully God, or conversely, in being found only in appearance as a man, Christ was not fully human. This is not the case. What this passage calls attention to is the glory of the pre-Incarnate Christ in contrast with the humility and servanthood of the Incarnated Christ.[28] Much of what we understand about the Incarnation is steeped in mystery. Years and years of debate, scholarly research, and writing have culminated in the soundness of a doctrine that puts forth that Christ was indeed both fully God and fully man. How this is possible is a mystery and only possible through the power of the divine Godhead.

What is most striking is Christ's descent and ascent. He goes down before he comes back up. He lowers himself before he is raised up. Christ's humility and servant nature bring him exaltation and glory. It is Christ's descent—his humility, obedience, and willingness to take human form—that we are called to imitate. By the world's system the only way to greatness is by our own prideful self-promotion. By God's system, only those that humble themselves are worthy of honor. It is a backward system to many, but it is God's system. And it is the system we are called to live by.

In Genesis, we found that we were *made in his image* and that we *bear his image*. In this passage, and throughout the writings of the New Testament, we are called to *be conformed to his image*. Listen to Paul:

"Your attitude should be the same as that of Christ Jesus." (2:5)
"Continue to work out your salvation with fear and trembling." (2:13)
"It is God who works in you to will
and to act according to his good purpose." (2:13)
This is not about you.
Whatever your ministry,
Whatever title you hold,
whatever honor you receive,
whatever beauty you create,
whatever blessings you have . . .
They are all because of him. They are for his honor and glory alone.

Be mindful of your attitude about these things. Keep Christ—his obedience, humility, and servanthood—in the forefront of your mind. Seek to imitate him. Conform yourself to him.

Later in Philippians, Paul writes that all his endeavors, all his accomplishments, all he's done to prove himself holy and worthy, are nothing. Read Philippians 3:7–14. Can you hear the passion in Paul's voice? In verse 10, he indicates that he will go as far as death in order to be conformed to the image of Christ! He wants to share in the suffering of Jesus Christ in order to be resurrected with him. What are you willing to give up so that Christ can be exalted? Christ gave up everything! To what degree could you do the same? What if he asked you to give up your ministry, your artwork, your creative voice?

I spoke briefly about my vocal cord surgery earlier. Through much of that experience, I knew I had to be obedient in giving up my role as a worship leader. I was willing to do that. What truly broke my heart most was the possibility of not being able to sing ever again. "How can I worship you without song, without voice, God?" my soul cried out in desperation. What I didn't realize in the midst of my fear was that he was teaching me to worship him in a new way—from the depths of my soul, without words, without song, without verbal voice. In that place of surrender, God allowed a new song of praise to rise up in me. It was an extremely difficult season of being conformed to his image. I'd never ask to repeat it, but I'd certainly never give it up.

Lord, conform us to your image.
  Let us decrease so you can increase.
    More of you, Lord, and less of me.
      More of you in my life, in my church, in my home, in my ministry.
    May I be your humble, obedient, and willing servant, Lord.
                    In your most blessed Name, amen.

Listen to: "Mansion" by Rita Springer

Digging Deeper:
All Things New

Read: Revelation 21

nother incredible passage of Scripture indeed! Can you imagine? The Holy City prepared as a beautiful bride! No more tears, death, mourning, or pain! All things made new! This is not just a duplication of earth as we know it, but a whole new creation. The Greek word for "new" is *kainon*, which indicates something that is "qualitatively new." Creation will have a new quality to it. What this means exactly will remain a mystery until that day, but it is certainly fun to imagine what it might be like.

The words of Genesis 1 and John 1 resonate throughout this passage as well. We find a creation story once again. We find God dwelling once more among his people—God restoring the relationship that he intended for his people. Except this time, it's not "in the beginning." It's "in the end." At the end of all time, God will restore all that has been destroyed at the enemy's hand.

While this passage may reflect a future reality, it also speaks of a present reality. Verse 6 indicates that it is already done. Christ has *already* risen triumphantly. The water of life is *already* available without cost. We are *already* children of God. We have *already* received our inheritance as his children. Paul tells us: "Therefore, if anyone is in Christ, he is a new creation; the old has gone, the new has come!" (2 Cor 5:17). All of these statements reveal a present-day reality for those who have chosen a life of faith in Jesus Christ.

We have *already* been made new!
We *will* be made new!
Present
Future

Many of us live for the future. We look forward to the perfection and restoration of all creation. Believe me, I eagerly anticipate this as well. But we must also remember that Christ perfects and restores *today*. Christ proclaimed from the cross: "It is finished!" (John 19:30). And indeed it is! We must stand triumphant with our Risen Lord.

Many of you may be at this very moment traversing a very difficult path in your earthly journey. The valley may be dark, the mountain dangerously steep, the desert very dry. Do not give up. Desperately seek to overcome. Christ is already triumphant. He is the Alpha and the Omega, the beginning and the end. His hand is already extending a drink from the spring of the water of life. Many of you might be thinking, "Yeah right! I am thirsting to death here. How can I get a drink when I don't even know where the fountain is right now?" Believe me. I know. I've been there. To say "It's not easy" is a gross understatement and belittles your pain. But notice: Christ *extends his hand to you.* "To him [or her] that is thirsty *I will give* . . ." (21:6, emphasis added). It doesn't say that you have to go to him. He comes to you. In the darkest, toughest, driest places, it is so hard to recognize the Lord's hand. But do not doubt—it is there!

Go with me on a mental journey for a minute. Picture yourself on the largest desert you can imagine. There is nothing in sight but sand—in all directions, sand. You have dropped to the ground, unable to go any further. You are parched. You feel as though you are dying. You pass out from thirst and exhaustion. Then, Christ comes to you. He kneels in the sand and cradles your head gently in his lap. From nowhere he produces a crystal clear glass of water. He lovingly dips the hem of his brilliant, white robe into the glass. He gently brings it to your burnt lips and allows the water to drip into your mouth. Slowly, your body absorbs the water so vital to life. He continues until every last drop is gone. Another glass appears. This continues—perhaps for a very long time. But he is there, the whole time, providing the water necessary to keep you alive.

Christ promises to make all things new. From the darkest, toughest, driest places, new life will spring. Jesus said: "I tell you the truth, unless a kernel of wheat falls to the ground and dies, it remains only a single seed. But if it dies, it produces many seeds" (John 12:24).

> Listen to his voice saying . . .
> "Behold! I make all things new!"
> *All things!*

Lord, I pray that you will extend your beautiful hand of mercy to your children reading this. I pray fervently for those who are thirsty, tired, exhausted, uncertain, and doubting. For those who have lost their faith; for those in the darkest of valleys, the driest of deserts—refresh them Lord with your Living Water.

Nurturing Creator, loving Father, bring light where there is darkness, freedom where there is bondage, life where there is death.

Like the caterpillar in its quiet cocoon, wrap them in your love so that they can emerge beautiful and strong.

We love you, Lord.

I pray this in Jesus' powerful and precious Name, amen.

Listen to: "All Things New" by Nicol Sponberg

Endnotes

1. Duckworth, "Incarnate Word," 39.
2. Peterson, *Christ Plays*, 87.
3. Langmead, *Word Made Flesh*, 15.
4. Ibid., 16.
5. Dunn, "Incarnation," 3:397–98.
6. This interpretation is found in more modern theological thought. I have taken the idea of the Incarnation as the birth, life, death, and resurrection of Christ from the work of Ross Langmead.
7. Langmead, *Word Made Flesh*, 19.
8. Thompson, *Incarnate Word*, 41.
9. Peterson, *Word Made Flesh*, 86.
10. Hart, "Through the Arts," 17.
11. Langmead, *Word Made Flesh*, 28.
12. Savage, "Through Dance," 74.
13. Hart, "Through the Arts," 20–21.
14. Langmead, *Word Made Flesh*, 56.
15. Begbie, *Voicing Creation's Praise*, 226–27.
16. Langmead, *Word Made Flesh*, 56.
17. We see some of this reflected in the epistles of Paul, although Paul was referring more to our carnal nature than our physical flesh. For an expanded discussion of this, see ibid., 25–29.
18. Savage, "Through Dance," 70.
19. Batz, "Embodying Praise," 2.
20. Lewis, *Mere Christianity*, 91.
21. Foster, *Streams*, 237.
22. Begbie, *Voicing Creation's Praise*, 82.
23. VerEecke, "A Vision," 144.
24. Hagner, *Word Biblical*, 17.
25. Her beautifully inspiring work can be seen at www.maryanneradmacher.com.
26. Sailhamer, *NIV Compact*, 552–53.
27. *Hebrew-Greek Key Word Study Bible*, 1381.
28. Ibid., 1676.

three

All Things Beautiful:
Towards a Theology of Beauty

" . . . to bestow on them a crown of beauty
instead of ashes . . ."

WATCHED AS THE band played quietly—notes softly rising, floating, across the huge stadium. On stage, a woman lay prostrate in grief at the foot of a large cross. Several people surrounded her. They lifted her gently from her sorrow and shame and gave her a robe of pure white. The lone singer's tender voice rang out across the auditorium as she sang a song based on these words found in Isaiah 61: "A crown of beauty for ashes." As she was lifted from the ashes of all that was lost, she was made new through Christ's suffering, redemption, and grace. Such was the scene at a worship event I attended with my daughter. As I watched the drama unfold, I was reminded once again of the passage where the promises of the coming Messiah are foretold: a crown of beauty instead of ashes, the oil of gladness instead of mourning, and a garment of praise instead of a spirit of despair. I was reminded of the beauty of the cross.

What Is Beauty?

In a world where physical appearance is both held on an undue pedestal and yet said to be "in the eye of the beholder," how do we as Christian artists define beauty? I am not just speaking of the physical appearance of a person, but also of the things around us. The way a piece of furniture has good lines; the way an architect designs a structure in congruity with its environment (think Frank Lloyd Wright); the way an artist captures the essence of his subject; the crystal clear voice of the trained opera singer— all those things in which beauty plays a role in defining how it is we see artistic creations around us. Is there a "theology of beauty" that helps us, as *Christian* artists, as *sacred* artists, see God in all of creation—both things created by the hand of God and those objects created by humanity through the imagination placed in us by our Creator? Be patient as we tease this out.

Father Robert VerEecke is a Jesuit priest whom I've had the pleasure of meeting on my journey of exploring creativity and movement in worship. Known as the "dancing priest," he teaches sacred dance through Boston College and utilizes dance and movement in masses at the Church of St. Ignatius of Loyola located by the BC campus. In his essay "A Vision of a Dancing Church," he provides some insight into a starting definition of beauty. Out of a personal experience, he writes of a "magical beauty" found in his former dance teacher:

> There was a quality about her movement that I can only describe as "spiritual"; it was ethereal and visibly transcendent. There was etched on her face and in her eyes the vision of a reality beyond the present moment but rooted in it. And yet it was strangely clear that the beauty of this moment was conceived in the deep expression of human agony. This perception of the transcendent so firmly root- ed in the enfleshed experience of struggle in this one life, enabled me to say: "This moment is clearly from God." It was a perception of the beauty of the human and divine not in competition, not looking for escape from each other, but simply merging as one.[1]

We find in this statement a sense of the godly divine intertwined with the human story of struggle as a beginning definition of the essence of true beauty—not a superficial appearance of gloss, but of God's glory revealed in the human condition.

Beauty from Pain

When I think of beauty, I am immediately reminded of two men I watched sing in *Britain's Got Talent*, a competition similar to *America's Got Talent* here in the U.S.[2] The first gentleman is Paul Potts, an unassuming cell phone salesman who claims that music was his best friend growing up. The other is a thirteen-year-old young man named Andrew Johnston. Both Paul and

Andrew sing opera. As they take the stage for their respective auditions in a theater filled with thousands, they look self-conscious and nervous. When they announce they are there to sing opera, the judges raise their eyebrows in amusement and disbelief.

Yet, as they begin to sing, the judges and the audience are mesmerized. It isn't long before the audience is on its feet cheering them on enthusiastically. Both singers indicated that they have been bullied—Paul as a youngster and Andrew now as a young teen. What is so mesmerizing in both of these men is that the divine beauty of their voices is rooted in the human story of their pain and struggle of being rejected and taunted. In their pain, they have used their singing as a means, not of escaping, but of meeting with the divine within themselves.

I am unaware whether either of these men believe in God or have a relationship with a saving Christ, but there is something very sacred in the gift they bring when they open their mouths to sing. There is something transcendent born out of pain that reflects the glory of God and *his* amazing beauty. It causes one to pause and realize that there is a truth that emanates from them as they do what God has indeed uniquely created them to do. As you watch the audience's reactions to them, you realize that there is something universal about the simplicity and depth of their gift of beauty.

We witness these simple, average people taking the stage to sing, and we expect it to be average like them (if not downright awful, truth be told). Yet as their first notes ring out across the auditorium, the sound is clear and oh so beautiful. It shocks us, intrigues us, and beckons us to hear, to really listen. In these simple, unassuming men we see ourselves—all the gifts we have to offer that have been shoved down and pushed aside by our fear of others and by the lies of the enemy.

Our spirits rise as Paul and Andrew give their gift of beauty—of the divine. We watch as the audience stands in recognition that something truly amazing, truly divine, is occurring in that very moment—a moment clearly from God. We watch as they joyously applaud, cheering them on, many with tears streaming down their faces, touched by the incredible, transcendent beauty they are witnessing. We hear in Paul's and Andrew's voices the ridicule, shame, and pain that they have endured from others who have mocked the beauty within them. And we discover that this incredible thing of beauty is born out of pain. Their pain was the stimulus that drove them to sing, and now the former place of pain is now a place of beauty as they sing.

Author Madeleine L'Engle makes this profound observation of artists and their dual pursuit of suffering and beauty:

> There is no denying that the artist is someone who is full of questions, who cries them out in great angst, who discovers rainbows in the darkness and then rushes to canvas or paper. An artist is someone who cannot rest, who can never rest as long as there is one suffering creature in this world. Along with Plato's divine madness there is also divine discontent, a longing to find the melody in the discords of chaos, the rhyme in the cacophony, the surprised smile in time of stress or strain."[3]

My friend Sally Tharp is a talented artist. She openly confesses,

> I am often drawn to the old, marred, scarred, and imperfect things in life, feeling the need to show a side of them that is beautiful, giving them a voice. The objects I choose to paint hold an aesthetic beauty to me and I paint them in that light. I invite the viewer to experience the qualities in them that I find appealing and to seek the beauty in the often overlooked, sometimes imperfect items of life."[4]

Are we discovering the beginning of a theology of beauty—true, deep, lasting beauty?

Beauty from Ashes

We cannot continue, however, without first turning to the example set by Jesus Christ. Author and theologian Jeremy Begbie proposes that a true theology of beauty is not based on "some formal principle from the contingent processes of the created world, but by directing our attention first of all to the redeeming economy of God that culminates in Jesus Christ."[5] According to Begbie, "In his earthly life, the beauty of Jesus was inward and hidden, but in his risen life, it is displayed in all its splendour, and is now revealed through those who follow him. Beauty therefore must now be understood in the light of Jesus Christ, through whom all things were created, an in whom creation is restored to its intended beauty."[6]

When Jesus returned from his wilderness temptation, he began his public ministry with a simple yet profound proclamation made at the synagogue in Nazareth (Luke 4:14–30). When he stood to read he declared his sacred mission—the very thing that God had uniquely created him to do—he read a portion of the passage found in Isaiah 61:1–3:

The Spirit of the Sovereign LORD is on me,
because the LORD has anointed me
to preach good news to the poor.
He has sent me to bind up the brokenhearted,
to proclaim freedom for the captives
and release from darkness for the prisoners,
to proclaim the year of the LORD's favor
and the day of vengeance of our God,
to comfort all who mourn,
and provide for those who grieve in Zion—
to bestow on them a crown of beauty
instead of ashes,
the oil of gladness
instead of mourning,
and a garment of praise
instead of a spirit of despair.
They will be called oaks of righteousness,
a planting of the LORD
for the display of his splendor.

Of course, the people mocked him, for that's what the enemy does—he uses people and lies to bring us down at the very moment we are trying to do what God has designed us to do. The Gospel records that Jesus only read the first of the three verses above, but as we read on in this passage, we find the promise of beauty. Out of our ashes—those places that the enemy has tried to destroy, the places we have mourned and cried tears over—Christ will bestow on us a crown of beauty. Beauty born out of pain—beauty from ashes. And to what end, for what purpose? For *the display of God's glorious splendor*—so God can show off through us!

The cross of Christ was also a place of ridicule, shame, and pain, yet it now stands as a place of beauty for all who will receive it. In his book *A Scandalous Beauty*, author Thomas Schmidt writes of the scandalous nature of the cross. He explains:

> So revolting was the concept of crucifixion to first-century audiences that the word rarely occurs in Roman literature, and when it does, it is often in plays involving the crude speech of slaves. In these sources, the cross is called variously *the tree of shame, the criminal wood,* and *the infamous stake.* . . . Thus crucifixion became an insult, a word of cursing, and there was even an accompanying hand signal. To give someone the sign of the cross in the first century had precisely the opposite purpose that it would have today.[7]

Yet in that scandal, there is beauty, redemption, and power over sin, death, and hell. In that place of rejection and scorn, Christ became one with the depths of humanity and wrestled there in that place until he rose victoriously three days later. Yet, according to Bruce Herman even "the ascended Christ still bears earthly wounds," and now stands as a wounded and broken beauty.[8]

Through the cross and resurrection, we are invited to become one with the Divine—there in this place our shame is overridden by the beauty of the power of the cross. There, as we face our own pain, we join Christ in the fellowship of sharing in his sufferings (Phil 3:10), and our suffering is turned into a thing of beauty where God's glory radiates from a heart that is transformed into the likeness of Christ (Ps 34:5; 1 Pet 1:6–7). I believe that the most beautiful creations of humanity are those that are born out of pain. There is something reflected in the glory of it that resonates in the human heart—something we recognize unconsciously. Somehow we realize this beauty born out of pain, the beauty from ashes. Somehow it connects us to the Divine. Even when we might choose not to believe or acknowledge God, his glory cannot be denied.

Glory or Gloss

I wrote earlier in this chapter about Robert VerEecke ("Father Bob") of Boston College. I spent two weeks studying with him and a group of other participants, exploring sacred dance and embodied prayer. At the end of the two weeks of study, class participants were invited to dance at the Feast of St. Ignatius service held at the parish. I was very touched throughout the service, and there were many times when my eyes were brimming with tears. I was deeply struck by the beauty of both the service itself, as well as all the different faces that encircled Father Bob as he lifted the bread and cup towards heaven at the altar as he blessed the sacraments: faces of all colors, nationalities, and shapes; male and female; faces marked by both youth and age; and even a face marked by Down's Syndrome. The diversity was amazingly beautiful—how it might look one day around the throne of God in heaven.

Father Bob's homily that day was entitled "Glory or Gloss." He spoke first of the glory of God evident in the lives of those who live according to God's purposes for their lives. Following the word *glory* in the dictionary is the word *gloss*. Unlike glory, gloss is a superficial shine that merely covers the surface of an object. Father Bob challenged the congregation to live above a life of superficial gloss, and to reach for a life in which the glory of God radiates from a heart in alignment with and fulfillment of the unique plans and purposes that God has for each of us as individuals.

Ruth St. Denis was a pioneer in the modern dance movement in America. A contemporary of Isadora Duncan, she danced in the early part of the twentieth century. Martha Graham and Doris Humphrey were among her students. For her, dance was not an external mechanic learned through technique and training, but an external expressional of an inner reality. In her writings, we find this short poem:

> I have used my body
> As a gleaming sword
> To cut outlines of beauty
> On the mind of the world.[9]

For St. Denis, encouraging her audiences to experience a deeper fullness of the rich beauty in creation was embedded in her philosophy of dance as a performance art. Creating pieces of beauty was a deeply spiritual experience for St. Denis, as it should be for all dancers, performers, actors, musicians, painters, sculptors, and artists. To use both the practical tools of our art (whether our bodies, our medium, our voices, or our instruments) and the deep places of our struggle to "cut outlines of beauty on the mind of the world" allows God to use our creative abilities for his glory and not simply our own vain "gloss" or gain.

Digging Deeper into a Theology of Beauty

As we contemplate beauty, may we find ourselves struck by the beauty of God. May we see his beauty in both the people and places all around us. May the seemingly simple reveal a deeper divinity. May our senses, hearts, minds, and spirits be open to beauty as defined by God, not the world. May we be able to look beyond the superficial gloss of this world and see God's glory revealed in the simple, the unadorned, and even the ugly.

Dear God, great Creator of our eyes, minds, and hearts, help us see as you see. Give us your eyesight, your mind-sight, your heart-sight. Let us see the mysterious beauty that you see in others that we struggle to see. And may you be glorified. Amen.

Digging Deeper: All Things Beautiful

Esther 2: Beauty from Within

Exodus 31 & 38: Powerful Beyond Measure

Psalm 27: To Seek a Face of Beauty

Isaiah 53: The Beautiful, Suffering Servant

Revelation 4–5: Beauty Beyond Words

Digging Deeper:
Beauty from Within

Read: Esther 2:1–18

The story of Esther is a wonderful story of beauty, courage, humility, and redemption. The orphan child, Hadassah, elevated to the place of queen—a young beauty who caught the eye of all, most importantly the king. Let me take you back to the beginning of the story. King Xerxes had just spent 180 days flaunting his wealth among the people of his land. This lengthy show of opulence was followed by a seven-day banquet with lots of wine and festivities. Queen Vashti (Esther's predecessor) also hosted a banquet with all the women of the royal community. In the middle of her celebration, she was brought a message from the king, who had summoned her to his party to parade her beauty. Queen Vashti ignored his request. Frankly, I don't really blame her. The king interrupted her party just so he could show her off at his. Who wants to be paraded around like that? However, by ignoring his request, Vashti was ousted from the royal throne. It seems like both were filled with pride, and it got the best of them.

Later King Xerxes recalled that he had deposed his beautiful queen and ordered all the fair maidens brought to the palace so he could pick his favorite. A new parade for the king! Imagine all these young women vying for the king's attention. I'm sure there was a great deal of primping and fawning, as well as backbiting and jealousy. But who is finally rewarded with the crown? The quiet, unassuming beauty in the back—Esther. It reminds me of Cinderella and her cruel stepsisters getting ready for the ball. And we know in the end that the glass slipper fit the maid who worked among the cinders.

The passage tells us that Esther was fair of face and form, but we also realize her beauty emanated from a deeper place as well. While the other women were adorning themselves with magnificent robes, gold jewelry, and kohl makeup, Esther sought the counsel of Hegai, the king's eunuch—who would certainly know what would make the king take notice. Her wisdom, paired with her outer and inner beauty, elevated her to queen, and through her courageous yet humble actions the nation of Israel was saved.

When we judge beauty by some worldly standard, we become blinded to a deeper beauty that emanates from the essence of a person—whether that person would be judged outwardly beautiful or not. Consider this observation by Harold Best:

Not all people are physically beautiful. Some of us are downright ugly, but people fall in love with us anyway, don't they? We may whisper over our coffee that we cannot figure out what this person sees in that person, yet they are giddy in love, blinded to what we think we have the eyes for. But it is the other way around? Have their eyes been opened to what we are blinded to? Is there something at work that has emptied them of certain prerogatives, only to fill them with deeper one?[10]

Do you see what he's driving at? As Christian artists, we need to judge beauty with the mind of God. Yes, Esther *was* indeed beautiful by the world's standards, but it was her *inner beauty* that garnered the attention of others. I'm certain there were lots of beautiful women around her, but there was something different about Esther. We cannot look with worldly eyes, but with the eyes of God.

All men and women are created in the image of God. That means all people (not just us Christians) somehow reflect the nature and beauty of God. It may be harder to see in some than others, yet it is there just the same. As Christians it is up to us to set the example for others—we must both *reflect* God's beautiful image and *see* with his all-seeing eyes. We must reflect a deep inner beauty—the glory of God—that causes others to stop and take notice. We must also see beyond the surface of others and look for the image of God, even in our darkest enemy.

This week as you go about life, open your eyes.
Ask God to help you see with his vision.
Look into your spouse's eyes—do you see what God sees?
Over coffee with your best friend, ask God to reveal what *he* likes
about them.
In the checkout lane, ask God to reveal the inner beauty
of the tired clerk at the end of her eight-hour shift.
When you run into that person that rubs you the wrong way,
can you see past the irritation to see him as God does?
And your enemy—can you see the redeeming qualities
that God has placed in her?
When you are apt to judge, step back and judge with God's mind instead.

Oh God, gives us your eyes to see the world
and people around us as they really are—image bearers of the King.
Amen.
Listen to: "Everywhere" by Rita Springer

Digging Deeper:
Powerful Beyond Measure

Read: Exodus 31:1–11 & 38:22–23

In the movie *Akeelah and the Bee,* the main character, Akeelah, finds a poem on the mantel in her spelling bee tutor's (Dr. Larabee) home. This is the dialogue that occurs between the two characters as she reads the poem:

Akeelah: [quoting Marianne Williamson] "Our deepest fear is not that we are inadequate. Our deepest fear is that we are powerful beyond measure. We ask ourselves, 'Who am I to be brilliant, gorgeous, talented, fabulous?' Actually, who are you not to be? We were born to make manifest the glory of God that is within us. And as we let our own light shine, we unconsciously give other people permission to do the same."

Dr. Larabee: Does that mean anything to you?

Akeelah: I don't know.

Dr. Larabee: It's written in plain English. What does it mean?

Akeelah: That I'm not supposed to be afraid?

Dr. Larabee: Afraid of what?

Akeelah: Afraid of . . . me?[11]

Why *are we* afraid of "me"? Why do we shy away from the person God created us to be?

Today's Scripture passage is very revealing. It holds both mystery and understanding for the Christian artist. Follow along with me. First, notice God's intentions and actions:

"I have chosen . . ."
"I have filled him with the Spirit of God . . ."
"I have filled him with skill, ability, and knowledge . . ."
"I have appointed . . ."
"I have given skill . . ."

God has a purpose and a plan for these two men. He has deliberately called and equipped them for a very special job. They are to help Moses build the tabernacle where the Israelite nation will worship their one true God, Yahweh. And they will do it just as God commanded it be done.

This is one of the first times in Scripture that we see God filling someone with his Spirit (Hebrew: *ruah*) in order to do something. We see this happening on various occasions throughout Scripture when the Spirit of God empowers people to do his work. Most often it is a prophet who is being filled; but here, in this case (one of the first cases), God is filling an artist, a craftsman, with his *Ruah*—his Breath, his Wind, his Creative Essence. According to Richard Foster, "The crucial point for us to see is this: God chose a skilled artisan and had him use his artistry to show forth God's manifest presence to his people. Bezalel worked as an artisan—this was his job, his profession—and it was through his vocation that he was to demonstrate the presence of God."[12] Bezalel, with Oholiab at his side, created a tabernacle that would be the center of their worship—the place where God's people would meet together in his manifest presence—for the next three hundred years!

Second, the word *ruah* is first used in Genesis 1:2 when the earth was still formless, empty, and void. Here we find the Spirit (*ruah*) of God hovering over the face of the earth. In the next verses that same Spirit begins creating. It is also used similarly in Job 26:23, "By his breath [*ruah*] the skies became fair," and in Psalm 33:6, "By the word of the LORD were the heavens made, their starry host by the breath [*ruah*] of his mouth." In these scriptures the *Ruah* of God is the great creating Spirit who with one breath breathes life into creation and with one thought imagines the world and it is so.

God still fills his artisans with his Spirit today in order to make known his glorious presence. He does this through the craft and creativity with which he has gifted us. He equips us with a variety of skills and talents, and he equips us to varying degrees. Notice that Oholiab was appointed by God to *assist* Bezalel. He also equipped him with different skills than Bezalel. All this was for a reason and a purpose. Some of us are called to be professional artists; others serve our churches or communities as laypersons. Some are to be in charge; others are meant to serve and follow instructions. Some of us are highly skilled in one particular area; others are jacks-of-all-trades. And it is *all* for *God's* glory. When we hold back, when we don't give our gift, others do not get to experience the presence of God in us that God intended for his glory. We do no service to others or to God when we withhold that which is placed within us.

We all have a gift to bring. Part of being an artist is figuring out what that gift is and in what context it is to be given. So, ask yourself:

What is my gift?

How is it unique or different?

Am I a professional or a hobbyist?

Given that, to what purpose is God using this gift?

Where is my gift to be given? To whom?

My friend Robert Wesner is artistic director of Neos Dance Theatre. He performs in both secular and sacred contexts. In both arenas, he is amazing to watch. I have seen him and his wife Brooke dance to the theme of the prodigal. It was profound and so beautiful to watch as the prodigal (Brooke) ran into the strong, open arms of her Father (Robert). He also is very connected to the dance ministries of the local churches in this region. He is often a guest artist at the workshops that I help organize. It is equally amazing as you watch this professional give his gift to the laypersons who dance in their local churches. When Robert gives his gift, he shines. When he teaches others to give their gift, it allows them to shine. *All* makes known the manifest presence of God.

In the same way, we need to discover our gifts and give them away. Only then can God be made known to those who cannot see or believe otherwise. Consider your gift. Ask God how he wants to use that gift. Be patient as you wait for him to reveal his plan to you. Be open to his filling, to his *Ruah*, to his instructions, to his voice. May God shine brilliantly and radiantly through you and your gift.

Listen to: "Fill Me Now" by Kim Hill
and "In Christ Alone" by Keith Getty

Digging Deeper:
To Seek a Face of Beauty

Read: Psalm 27

Think on this statement a moment:

> Only eyes trained by gazing continually toward the cross—
> only eyes cleansed by that second innocence,
> childlike habitual charity—can see true beauty, true goodness.[13]

That takes our first meditation to a whole new level now. It forces us to face the question: How can we see the beauty, the attributes, the nature of God in others if we don't know his beauty, attributes, or nature firsthand?

The word "gaze" in this passage is the Hebrew word *hazah*, which means "to see, look, behold, observe, or gaze." This is not a casual glance. It means to *really* look. There is also a prophetic nature to this word. Prophets would also use this same word to describe a vision or a dream. Job used this word when he spoke confidently about seeing the Lord when he died:

> I know that my Redeemer lives,
> and that in the end he will stand upon the earth.
> And after my skin has been destroyed,
> yet in my flesh I will see God;
> I myself will see him with my own eyes—I, and not another.
> How my heart yearns within me! (Job 19:25–27)

There is a confidence that underlies this word. It is to look at the unseen face of a mysterious God and still see with spiritual eyes.

There have been times in my life when I "lost sight" of God—not that I forgot about him or wasn't looking for him, but that my circumstances seemed to blind me to the fact that he was with me all the time. I would cry out to him and see no answers:

> "God, what are you doing?"
> "Where are you?"
> "Why can't I see you, God?"

But it was in those very times that he was right there beside me teaching me about patience, timing, and his ultimate goodness. He was teaching me to trust him, to wait on him, to take courage in him alone. I have so much to learn about God, and this side of heaven I will never truly know him. For now I see in a mirror dimly, but *then* I will see face to face! I long for that day, just as Job did. But every day—*right here on earth*—he is trying to reveal himself to me in tiny and mysterious ways, if only I had eyes that would see!

We must keep our eyes fixed on God:

> My eyes are fixed on you, O Sovereign LORD;
> in you I take refuge—do not give me over to death. (Ps 141:8)

Our eyes fixed on Christ:

> Let us fix our eyes on Jesus, the author and perfecter of our faith,
> who for the joy set before him endured the cross,
> scorning its shame,
> and sat down at the right hand of the throne of God. (Heb 12:2)

As you read Psalm 27 in its entirety, do you hear the distress in David's voice? Yet he chooses to trust in the Lord. He reminds himself to look into the face of God and to continue to seek after him. He remembers God's goodness and promises and chooses to place his trust in God—his light, salvation, and stronghold.

As we look into the face of God, of Christ, we learn about him: his goodness, his faithfulness, his love, his grace, his mercy, his sovereignty. In the very moments that we feel he has abandoned us, we must leave the lie of the enemy behind and look directly into the face of Christ:

> Turn your eyes upon Jesus,
> Look full in his wonderful face,
> And the things of earth will grow strangely dim,
> In the light of his glory and grace.[14]

Lord, help us. In our weakness, help us. We are easily distracted. We lose focus. We lose sight of your goodness, your promises, your faithfulness. Jesus didn't even turn his face from the shame of that dreadful cross, yet we turn away again and again from the beautiful face of our Savior. Help us to seek after you, *continually* seek after you. Open our eyes. Help us see the unseen.

In the Name of our Savior who never lost sight, amen.

Listen to: "Turn Your Eyes upon Jesus" by one of your favorite artists

Digging Deeper:
The Beautiful, Suffering Servant

Isaiah 52:13—53:12

This scripture is known as the passage of the *Suffering Servant*. It is a prophetic text spoken by Isaiah that looks to the Christ (or Anointed One) as the man who would be wounded so we could find healing. Isaiah has spoken earlier of God's servant as the nation of Israel, but the servant Israel has failed God. So Isaiah prophesies a new servant who will not fail. Read Isaiah 42:1–9. This is Isaiah's first prophecy about the Servant who will come as a light to all nations. Together, these two passages paint a picture of the servant role that Christ would take. The verses in Isaiah 42 point towards Christ's ministry on earth, while the passage that starts at the end of Isaiah 52 looks towards the passion of Christ and the glory of his resurrection.

What is interesting about these passages is the references to the appearance of Christ. We find here a man without beauty—at least as the world defines it. We also come face to face with a man who would be marred and disfigured as he took on the sins of the people. After his resurrection, when Christ appeared to his disciples, he still bore the scars of his crucifixion. Christ appeared to Thomas, and said, "Put your finger here; see my hands. Reach out your hand and put it into my side. Stop doubting and believe" (John 20:27). A Victorious Warrior with battle wounds! While we admire the handsome and beautiful among us, Christ puts forth an image that opposes our conception, or rather misconception, of beauty.

Christ's disfigurement stands in opposition to the fact *we* are now without blemish. His wounds lead to our healing. His brokenness makes us whole. His death brings us life. In Christ, we are redeemed and all of creation is restored. Consider this statement by Jeremy Begbie: "In his earthly life, the beauty of Jesus was inward and hidden, but in his risen life, it is displayed in all its splendor, and is now revealed through those who follow him. Beauty therefore must now be understood in the light of Jesus Christ, through whom all things were created, and in whom creation is restored to its intended beauty."[15]

The prophet Habakkuk writes of the radiant scars of Christ:

> His coming is as brilliant as the sunrise.
> Rays of light flash from his hands,
> where his awesome power is hidden. (3:4, NLT)

In Christ's nail-pierced hands, his power is made manifest. Even though man would shun the one who died as a criminal on a tree, it is in that death and its accompanying scars that his true power is hidden. For it is only in his hands—driven through by nails—that we find healing, peace, and forgiveness. It is there we find his true and awesome power.

Tomorrow we will read in Revelation of the risen and glorified Christ, but today we are reminded that he was mocked, beaten, scourged, whipped, and spat upon—that his hands and feet were nailed to a tree, and his side was pierced.

> When I survey the wondrous cross on which the Prince of glory died,
> My richest gain I count but loss and pour contempt on all my pride.
> Forbid it, Lord, that I should boast, save in the death of Christ my God!
> All the vain things that charm me most, I sacrifice them to his blood.
> See from his head, his hands, his feet, sorrow and love flow mingled down!
> Did e'er such love and sorrow meet or thorns compose so rich a crown?
> His dying crimson, like a robe spreads o'er his body on the tree;
> Then I am dead to all the globe and all the globe is dead to me.
> Were the whole realm of nature mine that were a present far too small;
> Love so amazing, so divine, demands my soul, my life, my all.[16]

Dear Lord and Savior Jesus Christ, your death reminds us that we live in a world that has been made imperfect by our sin. In your disfigurement, we are reminded that we can't always look to the outward appearance of a person or event—that not everything can be taken at face value. For behind the face that was mangled and beaten, there was and is a beauty that is beyond our comprehension. We are reminded that your blood and the water from your side flowed down as sorrow and love, and that your crown of thorns pierced your tender brow as you faced the scorn of a people that did not comprehend or receive you. Yes, Lord, the love you offer demands our souls, our lives, our all. We surrender ourselves, yet again, to you.

In your most precious Name we pray, amen.

Listen to: "The Wondrous Cross" by Chris Tomlin

Digging Deeper:
Beauty Beyond Words

Read: Revelation 4–5

Yesterday we read of the marred and disfigured Christ. Today we read of the same Christ now glorified. What is interesting about this passage is that Christ appears as a lamb that has been slain. Now we imagine this passage figuratively, and we know that this refers to the one who was willing to die sacrificially on behalf of the sins of the people. But what if we imagined this sight *literally*? I don't think it would be very pretty. It's hard to imagine what John really saw in his vision. I get the feeling that John could scarcely describe the vision of glory he had seen. When I read the passages above, I can hardly imagine what it was like. How can we imagine a rainbow that resembles an emerald encircling the throne? How can we imagine the four living creatures, like earthly creatures, but really quite different? It is apparent that he lacked words to describe.

The sacrificial lamb is also referred to as the Lion of the tribe of Judah—quite a different picture than a slain lamb. The text goes back thousands of years to the blessing spoken by Jacob over his son Judah in Genesis 49. It is generally accepted as a messianic prophecy referring to a descendant from the tribe of Judah, when the ruler's staff or scepter would one day return to the rightful King. The passage in Revelation finds the true and final Lion of Judah worthy to open the scroll. The scepter has returned to the Ruler of all heaven and earth.

> Your throne, O God, will last forever and ever;
> a scepter of justice will be the scepter of your kingdom. (Ps 45:6)
> The kingdom of the world has become
> the kingdom of our Lord and of his Christ,
> and he will reign for ever and ever. (Rev 11:15)

What a beautiful picture of worship painted here in Revelation! Throughout Revelation we find John using the things of this world—things we can feel, see, touch—to describe the indescribable. He also relies on ancient texts and traditions to help describe what he saw in his vision.

C. S. Lewis mimics this inability to describe heaven in his book *The Last Battle*. The final book in the Chronicles of Narnia series, it describes the end of time in Narnia, as well as the beginning of a whole new world with the mighty lion Aslan. Note how he describes the indescribable:

> It is hard to explain how this sunlit land was different than the old Narnia as it would be to tell you how the fruits of that country taste. Perhaps you will get some idea of it if you think like this. You may have been in a room in which there was a window that looked out on a lovely bay of the sea or a green valley that wound away among mountains. And in the wall of that room opposite to the window there may have been a looking-glass. And as you turned away from the window you suddenly caught sight of that sea or that valley, all over again, in the looking-glass. And the sea in the mirror, or the valley in the mirror, were in one sense just the same as the real ones: yet at the same time they were somehow different—deeper, more wonderful, more like places in a story: in a story you have never heard but very much like to know. The difference between the old Narnia and the new Narnia was like that. The new one was a deeper country: every rock and flower and blade looked as if it meant more. I can't describe it any better than that: if you ever get there you will know what I mean.[17]

John's descriptions in Revelation are much like this—truly a picture of glory, beauty, and restoration—deeper than anything we could imagine. And one day, when we get there, we'll know what he means.

As artists we do the same thing as the disciple John and the writer C. S. Lewis. We take our life's experiences, our traditions, the things we've seen and witnessed, and we draw on those things to help us describe the indescribable. Laura Story's song "Indescribable" tries to use words to describe that which cannot be described. Do you see the irony in that? She draws on nature and life to explain what cannot be explained. As Story reveals how the song came about, we see her wrestling with the indescribable nature of God:

> I was driving through the mountains of North Carolina, admiring the blue haze of each mountain and the unique form of each tree and leaf. Psalm 19 tells us that the heavens declare the glory of God, and on that day, God was truly nourishing my soul with the beauty of his creation. My first inclination was to sing, but initially, no words came to mind. And that's when I started to consider how indescribable God is. What words could mere humans give to express his grandeur? Any praises we lift to him are our feeble attempts at capturing a small glimpse of the magnitude of who God is.[18]

As Christian artists, we struggle in much the same way.

We are at a loss for words. Emotion and color and sound and images flash across our hearts, minds, and souls, and somewhere deep in our spirit, if we are open to it, we finally find voice to describe our own vision of God. Even now I am pressed to understand the emotions that well up inside me. I just know that we, as artists, are here on this earth for a reason. All the scholarship and knowledge and theology and thoughts in the world still fall short in describing who he is. As artists, we are here to reveal God's glory. God has called and equipped us to tell of his glory and mercy and love. None of us can tell the story alone—we simply reveal a glimpse of God and his incredible, indescribable nature.

Lord, I pray that you will give us the voice, the words, the colors, the images, the movements, the sounds we need to describe you in all your glory. Give us a voice to describe. Help us tell your story. We are weak, earthen vessels, unable to contain all of who and what you are. Through our weakness, be strong. Tell the world who you are. We are your conduits. Help us get out of the way. More of you and less of us, Lord. May your glory be revealed through all of creation. Lord, fill us with more. Use our imaginations. Reveal yourself in brilliance and radiance as we struggle to find the words. May we be ever mindful that we can never contain you, that all we can say or paint or dance or sing or create will never be enough. Lord, one day, when we get there, we'll know fully, just as we on this earth have been fully known.

In the Name of the glorious one seated on the throne, amen.

Listen to: "Indescribable" by Laura Story
and "Revelation" Song by Jennie Lee Riddle

Endnotes

1. VerEecke, "A Vision," 143.
2. Both Paul Potts and Andrew Johnston and their amazing stories can be found on YouTube.
3. L'Engle, *Walking*, 168.
4. Quoted from Tharp's website, at http://sallytharp.com/about.
5. Begbie, *Voicing Creation's Praise*, 225.
6. Ibid., 97.
7. Schmidt, *Scandalous Beauty*, 49.
8. Herman, "Wounds and Beauty," 111.
9. St. Denis, "The Sword," as quoted in Douglas-Klotz, "Ruth St. Denis," 114.
10. Best, *Unceasing Worship*, 198.
11. Atchison, *Akeelah and the Bee*. The quote from Marianne Williamson is taken from her book *Return to Love*, 190–91.
12. Foster, *Streams*, 249.
13. Herman, "Wounds and Beauty," 119.
14. Helen H. Lemmel, "Turn Your Eyes upon Jesus," public domain, 1922.
15. Begbie, *Voicing Creation's Praise*, 97.
16. Isaac Watts, "When I Survey the Wondrous Cross," public domain, 1707.
17. Lewis, *Last Battle*, 195–96.
18. Story, "Story behind the Song."

four

The Priestly Role of the Artist

"You will be for me a kingdom of priests . . ."

Y FRIEND SARAH IS a writer and a poet. Recently at church she gave her testimony, which was rather like a confession. For years she sat in church and picked apart the service, noticing all the flaws and shortcomings. Then one day, she realized she had the attitude of a consumer, rather than a worshiper. The Holy Spirit convicted her to offer her gifts to the service rather than stand back and criticize it. Now both she and her husband are a vital part of our worship team, adding creativity and thoughtfulness to our worship services. She will sometimes read poems that augment our theme. One year, she wrote poems to accompany creative displays on the last seven words of Christ. Her words cause us to think, and sometimes rethink, how we see God and our relationship with him. They also resonate in our hearts and help us connect to deep places within. As she offers this gift, she is walking in her role as a priestly poet.

A Priestly History Lesson

Before we can understand our roles as priestly artists, we have to understand the role of priests in Scripture—where they came from, what they did, and what happened to them. So let's begin.

The first priest mentioned in the Bible is Melchizedek, found in Genesis 14. He was not a Levite, for he lived before Levi was even born. In fact, he wasn't even Jewish; he was the Canaanite king of Salem (later known as

Jerusalem). But Scripture clearly states he was a priest of *El-Elyon*, the Most High God. In this story we find him meeting Abraham and the king of Sodom in the Valley of Kings, following the battle in which Abraham rescued his nephew Lot, as well as these two kings and their nations. Melchizedek's gracious attitude stands in stark contrast to the king of Sodom's grudging one, and he recognizes that God's favor rests on Abraham. Instead of the simple, customary bread and water, Melchizedek brings bread and wine, the food of royalty and kings. He offers it to Abraham, along with a blessing. Abraham offers a tithe in return, which wasn't necessary but customary at the time, and it demonstrated Abraham's recognition of Melchizedek's role as priest and king.

The next priest mentioned in Scripture is Aaron, brother of Moses and Miriam, and he plays a crucial role beside Moses freeing the descendents of Abraham who now find themselves enslaved by the Egyptians. In Exodus 28 and 29 we see God's instructions for Aaron and his sons, as God moves them from solely prophet into the role of priests of the Hebrew people. But it isn't long before Aaron finds himself in trouble with a certain golden calf (Exod 32). When Moses discovers them worshiping the calf, he calls for all who would align themselves with God. The Levites (the tribe of Moses and Aaron) come forward only to be commanded to "strap a sword to [their] sides" and kill "brother, friend, and neighbor" (v. 27) to rid the camp of evil. These Levites are the descendents of Jacob's son Levi, who is linked to his brother Simeon as the sons who brought Jacob shame when they killed Shechem and his men as revenge for their defiled sister Dinah (Gen 34). On his deathbed, Jacob's "blessing" to these sons is more a curse, as he acknowledges their "swords as weapons of violence" and tells them they will be scattered throughout Israel (Gen 49:5–7). Now, here in Exodus, the swords that vengefully killed the men of Shechem become the swords that kill the men of Israel as God's revenge on those who've bowed down to the golden calf. The Levites obey God, and three thousand Israelites are killed that day. For their obedience, the Lord blesses them and sets them apart from the other tribes of Israel. Later when the Israelites are dividing the Promised Land, the Levites are scattered throughout the land to serve as priests—Abraham's "blessing" fulfilled.

Now fast forward several thousand years to Christ. The priests currently serving the Israelites are still decedents of Levi, according to Mosaic Law, which, of course, they still follow. But according to prophecy, the Messiah would come from the tribe of Judah through the line of David and serve as priest and king. Re-enter Melchizedek, the original priest of Scripture, whose name means "King of Righteousness." The same Melchizedek who ruled as king of Salem (now Jerusalem), which means "King of Peace." By this time, Melchizedek had a messianic interpretation due to his linkage to David in Psalm 110:4—King David was from the tribe of Judah (*not* Levi), but still called by God to serve as an honorary priest through his role as king. And the coming Messiah would serve "in the order of Melchizedek" and King David.

Further explanation is found in the book of Hebrews.[1] Melchizedek has no ancestry, lineage, birth, or death recorded in Scripture. In this manner, he serves as an archetype or model for a "continual priesthood"—one with no beginning or end—and has no connection to Mosaic Law. The writer of Hebrews goes to great lengths to explain why Christ's priesthood was "different and superior to Levitical priesthood," and according to scholar William Lane, "render[s] the Aaronic institution obsolete."[2] The writer of Hebrews presents Melchizedek not as a redeemer but as "a historical figure who serves as a precedent for a priesthood not based on lineage or law."[3] As we know, Christ came to abolish the law, but the Jewish Christians had a hard time letting go of that law.

Christ our Messiah is a descendant of Judah who serves in the same way as Melchizedek, as both our King and High Priest. Just as Melchizedek brought out the royal fare of bread and wine to Abraham, so too does Christ. Before his death, Christ serves the Passover bread and wine to his disciples. And every time we celebrate Communion, Christ still brings bread and wine to the table. Bread and wine—the food of royalty and kings. History comes full circle through our High Priest, Jesus Christ.

The "Set Apart" Priest—Then and Now

First and foremost, all of Israel was chosen by God to enter into a covenantal relationship. When God rescues them from slavery, we find him spelling out that covenant to the entire nation:

> Then Moses went up to God, and the LORD called to him from the mountain and said, "This is what you are to say to the descendants of Jacob and what you are to tell the people of Israel: 'You yourselves have seen what I did to Egypt, and how I carried you on eagles' wings and brought you to myself. Now if you obey me fully and keep my covenant, then out of all nations you will be my

treasured possession. Although the whole earth is mine, *you will be for me a kingdom of priests* and a holy nation.' These are the words you are to speak to the Israelites." (Exod 19:3–6, emphasis added)

So essentially, he was calling *everyone* to serve him as priests, not just the elect few holy enough to be fit for service. Even so, out of this kingdom of priests Aaron, his sons, and the Levites were "set apart" (Deut 10:8) to serve as leaders among this kingdom of priests. Many others were also "chosen and designated by name" (1 Chr 16:41) to lead the people in worship of God. So while *all are called* to be priests of God, there's still a hierarchy. Those who have proven themselves faithful are set apart as leaders (Num 17).

As Christians we are all part of this same kingdom of priests. Further, as artists and creative types you also are set apart, chosen, and designated by name to serve as priests within the kingdom of God. Some will serve like Levites in a supportive role, others in a more prominent role like Aaron. Still others, like Melchizedek, point God's people to their potential as priests and kings. Henri Nouwen, in speaking of the role of the Christian leader says, "He [or she] is a leader because he [or she] faces the world with eyes full of expectation, with the expertise to take away the veil that covers its hidden potential."[4] Is that not also the role of the artist and creative Christian? Through our creative work, we lift the veil and help make the invisible visible. That's what the arts do—they help us "see" things that are difficult to see, they help give us spiritual eyesight.

Theologian Jeremy Begbie talks about our role as "priests of creation," and he states: "The Son has taken flesh and, as it were, offered creation back to the Father in his own humanity, and now through the Holy Spirit invites us to share in the task of bringing creation to praise and magnify the Father in and through him."[5] According to Begbie, the "sensitivity of the artist" is necessary to help others see.[6]

Do you hear God calling you? Setting you apart? Choosing and designating you by name? No one has the same exact gift mix as you. Within the kingdom, you alone can bring the offering he's placed within you. Your creativity joins with creation and helps others see God. Just as mountains point to the grandeur of God and sunsets point to the beauty of God, your artwork and creativity point to the vast nature of God in so many varied and mysterious ways.

I understand many creative people don't see themselve as priests and leaders; they do not feel qualified. But God doesn't call the qualified; he qualifies the called. Again, Nouwen calls us as leaders in our giftings: "A Christian leader is a man [or woman] of hope whose strength in the final analysis is based neither on self-confidence derived from his [or her] personality, nor on specific expectations for the future, but on a promise made to him [or her]."[7] God instilled these creative gifts and talents in you for a reason, not just for your own pleasure or leisure. They were placed in you as a promise.

The "Consecrated" Priest—Then and Now

Throughout Exodus we find God's specific instructions for the ordination of the priests who would serve him (Exod 28–29, 40), and in Leviticus we see Moses carrying these instructions out (Lev 8). Throughout these passages we find two words often connected—*anoint* and *consecrate*.

- "Anoint Aaron and his sons and consecrate them so they may serve me as priests." (Exod 30:30)

- "Then dress Aaron in the sacred garments, anoint him, and consecrate him so he may serve me as priest. Bring his sons and dress them in tunics. Anoint them just as you anointed their father, so they may serve me as priests. Their anointing will be to a priesthood that will continue throughout their generations." (Exod 40:13–15)

- [Moses] poured some of the anointing oil on Aaron's head and anointed him to consecrate him. (Lev 8:12)

In these passages, Aaron and his sons were anointed in order to consecrate them to serve God. Likewise, the items placed in the tabernacle were anointed in order to consecrate them and be deemed holy before the Lord. Just as Aaron and sons served God, these items served God through their use in the worship and sacrifices of the Jewish people. Moreover, the anointing oil used in this consecration was a special sacred oil to be used only by God's specific instructions and never for personal use (Exod 30:22–33). God's instructions are very specific and to be followed just as he commanded. This wasn't a casual appointment, but a sacred, holy calling, and the ritual associated with it wasn't to be entered into offhandedly or carelessly. There was something about this ritual of anointing that consecrated God's people for service.

We often hear that a certain artist or ministry is *anointed*. While this doesn't mean that God literally comes down and pours oil over a person, figuratively he might indeed do that. Sometimes we see that symbolized by an anointing, consecration, or ordination service whereby a pastor or elder anoints a person in order to consecrate them to serve God. The idea behind this is that God still sets apart people for his service in a specific way today. It also doesn't mean that *every* artist or avenue of creativity is anointed to the same level or service. There was Aaron who served over all; there were the Levites who served in many, smaller ways; and there was an entire kingdom of priests called to being glory to his name. We have to understand at what level we are called to serve him.

God may be calling you to higher levels of service in his kingdom. He has specific ways in which he wants you to serve. And he will "anoint" you in order to consecrate you. To *consecrate* is to make or declare sacred, to set apart or dedicate to the service of God, or to devote or dedicate to some purpose. If someone has told you that you or your work is anointed, you better take heed. God is most likely calling you to a higher level of service and dedication to his kingdom. This also means a life of holiness. No longer can we actively engage in sinful lifestyles or follow the desires of our flesh. If we are truly anointed, God is declaring us sacred, set apart, and dedicated to his service.

The "Active" Priest—Then and Now

The priests and Levites had many roles in service to God and his tabernacle: consecrating all things holy; ministering before the Lord; pronouncing blessings; carrying and serving before the Ark of the Covenant; receiving and sacrificing offerings; making petitions before the Lord; giving thanks and praise; deciding on spiritual matters represented by the Urim and Thummin; expounding the Law of Moses; serving at local sanctuaries; and preparing the people for battle. In other words, there were many roles and responsibilities and many more people called to fulfill those roles! There was a great deal to be done, but God called many to his service to accomplish it.

Harold Best writes about the roles of the arts and the artist in worship today in his book entitled *Unceasing Worship*.[8] Let me draw out two vital points of his book as it relates to the priestly role of the artist. First, our art is an act of worship:

Christian artists, therefore, must understand from the start that their art, whatever its kind, venue, or quality, is as much an act of worship as is preaching the gospel. Knowing this first of all, before they pick up brush or chisel, is of supreme importance. The more Christian artists understand that artistic action is nothing other and nothing less than pouring perfume on Jesus' feet, the more they will be refreshed and liberated in their imagining and crafting.[9]

Second, while our art may work alongside preaching, Best points out that it can never take the place of it:

The arts should never take the place of direct proclamation. Rather, they should be used in worship as themselves, ultimately pointing away from themselves to the truth, but never giving the impression that they can do what truth alone can do. We must allow each artform, with its particular vocabularies and structures and contours to go directly to God in their purest form, uncluttered by our weak and untrusting spirits that get nervous if everything that we do does not shout John 3:16.[10]

Best makes two essential points here. First, any creative act done for the Lord is worship—whether that creative act is playing drums, acting in a drama, or writing a sermon. Whatever we do, if done for the glory of God, it is an act of worship. Second, while our creative arts may be just as much an act of worship as a sermon, it can't take the place of direct proclamation of God's word. The arts, music, and creativity are all to work alongside the sermon to proclaim the truth of God's covenantal love and Christ's saving grace and mercy.

I have heard it said that God does not *need* our worship. While we might argue that point, we must agree that he most certainly *deserves* it. And when we examine Scripture, we also see that he *commands* it. The jobs of the priests were not optional. God instituted them and rewarded his people for following them. Remember Christ did not come to abolish the law; he came to fulfill it (Matt 5:17). Christ serves as our perfect High Priest, and we are his royal priesthood (1 Pet 4:9). As his kingdom of priests, we were created to worship him, to magnify him, to proclaim his goodness and mercy. We were created to reflect his glory, to be light in a world that is filled with darkness. In the words of Madeleine L'Engle, "We are to be children of the light, and we are meant to walk in the light. . . . The creative act helps us emerge into the light."[11]

The many roles of the priests and Levites have been passed along to us. Examine the list at the beginning of this section, and ask yourself:

How can my art or creative act serve one of these roles?
How can my music minister to the Lord and his people?
How can my paintings pronounce blessing?
How can my poetry and prose bring thanks and praise to the Lord?
How can my dance prepare the people for battle?
How can I serve as a priest of the Lord Most High?
You are called to be an active priest. How will you serve?

The "Excellent" Priest—Then and Now

Leviticus 21 contains a slew of rules that the priests of ancient Israel had to follow—special haircuts, virgin brides, and defiled daughters thrown into the fire! In verses 16–23 we read that those born with a defect could not come near the food offerings. These rules may seem odd to us reading them today. In fact, by today's standards, where we are taught that people with disabilities are no different than those able-bodied, it might even seem harsh. Yet it served a definite purpose in that day among God's chosen people. I believe today they serve a different purpose. God deserves our highest praise. He is calling us, as his priests, to serve him with excellence. He doesn't want our leftovers and our defects. He wants our best.

In another story, found in Leviticus 10, we read of the death of Aaron's sons Nadab and Abihu. It also speaks to the excellence God demands of his servants. In this story, the two brothers have come drunk to the tabernacle and, in their confused state, they botch the special incense recipe causing an explosion that kills them both. Aaron's remaining sons, Eleazar and Ithamar, are anointed to take their place, and the Lord gives them strict rules about drinking before coming to serve. In this passage, God declares: "Among those who approach me, I will be proved holy; in the sight of all the people, I will be honored" (v. 3). Yes, God deserves our highest praise. He wants our best—clear minds, contrite hearts, and prepared spirits.

I know there are many arguments about quality and excellence in worship: professional vs. lay; paid vs. volunteers; trained vs. untrained; technicality vs. emotion; performance vs. worship—yes, we've all been pitted against one another. However, we cannot deny the biblical mandate to bring our very best. God *will be honored* in our praise and worship of him.

A great deal has been written about this topic of excellence. Harold Best admits that while God is able to see all our attempts at creative offerings through the perfecting lens of Jesus Christ, it doesn't excuse shoddy work: "We reside on the temporal side of the artistic action and are fully responsible for the content and intent. Thus it does no good to say that because God sees bad art though Christ we are absolved of responsibility for quality."[12] Best sees the artist and creative person in the church as ambassadors of God. He says, "We are ambassadors, forth-telling outpourers in everything we do, as if God himself is making his appeal through us. Yes, he uses the lowly things of this world to bring honor to him. But 'lowly' has a deeper meaning than 'mediocre' or even 'untrained.' 'Lowly' means meek, humble, quiet, whole and perhaps small, whereas 'mediocre' means tawdry, poorly structured, wasteful, irrespective of size, training or talent."[13]

An understanding congregation can overlook an awkward dance with a few mistakes performed by a group of untrained teens on Youth Sunday. But that may not be true of the many unchurched visitors who sit in our pews on Easter and Christmas. We must consider our audience.

I once watched a group of adults dressed in camo "marching" a very elementary dance (i.e., more appropriate for children) at an evening service packed with visitors. As the dance ended I pictured Jesus up in heaven looking down saying, "Oh, how cute!" Cute. Not glorious or beautiful or uplifting. Cute. A month or so later, I returned to a much smaller worship service at that same church where a woman danced prophetically throughout the service. While she wasn't a highly technical dancer, she was obviously gifted, anointed, and naturally very talented and graceful. I was overwhelmed by all that her danced revealed about the mysteries of God. I've also attended an African American service where three teens, also dressed in camo, did a hip-hop dance that blew the congregation away! They had obviously worked very hard, and they were great dancers. It was powerful and proclaimed Christ as mighty Warrior and King!

Some might claim their inspiration comes from God and overrides any need for the hard work that excellence requires. But inspiration, hard work, and excellence go hand in hand. "Inspiration does not do away with the need for strenuous, painstaking, and often frustrating effort. Quite the contrary, it is in just this kind of toil that the Spirit is probably most active," writes Jeremie Begbie.[14] This isn't about training for training sake, but about learning the intricacies of your talents and gifts so that you can give them back to the Lord in a way that honors him and brings him glory. Madeleine L'Engle adds these thoughts:

> The artist knows total dependence on the unseen reality. The paradox is that the creative process is incomplete unless the artist is, in the best and most proper sense of the word, a technician, one who knows the tools of his trade, has studied his techniques, is disciplined.
>
> . . . The moment of inspiration does not come to someone who lolls around expecting the gift to be free. It is no giveaway. It is the pearl for which we have to pay great price, the price of intense loneliness, the price of that vulnerability which often allows us to be hurt. . . . And I'm not sure if it's a choice. If we're given a gift—and the size of the gift, great or small, is irrelevant—then most of us must serve it, like it or not.[15]

As his priests, we must learn the tools of our trade. We must be thoroughly and thoughtfully prepared. We must understand that our "voice" is very powerful, and it should be powerfully trained. We must approach the Lord with excellence and quality, without defect or "drunkenness." Our God will be proven holy, and he will be honored in all that we bring him.

Digging Deeper into Your Priestly Role

Are you ready to join God's anointed? Those he's set apart to lead others in worship of him? Are you ready to be actively involved in worship? To work towards quality and excellence in the gift you offer? All of these are important questions to ask yourself as you consider your own priestly role as artist. Perhaps you lead worship or play in the band. Perform dances or dramas in your church; paint regularly for your services. Or perhaps you play for an audience of one in the privacy of your home. Paint, dance, create, and worship in the quiet of your studio. Perhaps you enjoy writing but aren't sure if anyone would want to read what you write. Perhaps you have walked in your priestly role for years without calling it that or stopping to consider the anointing God has placed on you and your ministry. Perhaps, like my poet friend Sarah, you've have sat in your pew unwilling to offer your gift. Perhaps you've offered your gift, only to have the church turn it away. Take a moment to examine your role, your creative gifts, your attitudes, your experiences.

Consider how God might be calling you to walk in your role as priest. Some will serve as Melchizedek in a more prophetic role. Some will serve as Aaron, leading the people at a crucial time in your church's history. Some will serve as Levites, supporting the worship service and all it entails to make it happen. Some will serve as Aaron's younger sons, waiting until others leave for you to fulfill your calling and anointing.

As you work through these studies, keep these thoughts and questions in mind. Listen to God's voice as you read.

Digging Deeper: The Priestly Role of the Artist

1 Peter 2: Chosen Royalty
1 Chronicles 16: Getting Our Priestly Praise On
Numbers 6: The Honor of the Priestly Blessing
Numbers 16: Standing in the Gap
Matthew 2: Wise Counsel to Kings

Digging Deeper:
Chosen Royalty

Read: 1 Peter 2:4–10

everal years ago our dance ministry visited the beautiful city of Barcelona, Spain. When we visited the Cathedral of the Holy Cross, it was undergoing a major facelift. Now we've all seen large buildings under renovation surrounded by scaffolding and construction tarps—not a very pretty or promising sight to say the least. Yet there in Barcelona, they had done something different. On the outside of the scaffolding the tarps depicted what the cathedral would look like when its facelift was complete. So while we couldn't see the cathedral in all its glory, we saw all that it was meant to be.

The same is true of the body of Christ. We can't see the church in the fullness of its true beauty or glory, but God sees all that it was meant to be. Christ serves as the cornerstone and foundation of the most incredibly beautiful temple. That temple, or "spiritual house" as Peter calls it, is built from the community of believers as "living stones" (v. 5). Yet we aren't perfect, and it sometimes seems as if we might never be built up into a thing of beauty. But just like the scaffolding covered in tarps with a picture of the future, God surrounds us, supports us, and shows everything we are meant to be.

The passage in 1 Peter contains one of the largest collections of references to the Old Testament. Peter begins with references to the priests, temple, and sacrifices of the Old Testament, but calls for a *new* priesthood, a *new* temple, and a *new* kind of sacrifice. Then, the three scriptures quoted are from Isaiah 28:16; Psalm 118:22; and Isaiah 8:14. These are followed by a powerful verse filled with words and promises of the past: "But you are a chosen people, a royal priesthood, a holy nation, God's special possession, that you may declare the praises of him who called you out of darkness into his wonderful light" (v. 9).

Note the four pairs of words—chosen people, royal priesthood, holy nation, special possession—and how they refer back to several key Old Testament scriptures:

- Now if you obey me fully and keep my covenant, then out of all nations you will be my treasured possession. Although the whole earth is mine, you will be for me a kingdom of priests and a holy nation. (Exod 19:5–6)

- "You are my witnesses," declares the Lord, "and my servant whom I have chosen. (Isa 43:10)

- For you are a people holy to the LORD your God. The LORD your God has chosen you out of all the peoples on the face of the earth to be his people, his treasured possession. (Deut 7:6; also very similar to Deut 14:2)

Also notice that just as Christ is chosen by God and precious to him, so too are we.

We are also called into a holy and royal priesthood.
Holy, set apart, consecrated.
Royal sons and daughters of King Jesus.

A royal priesthood like that of Melchizedek—both king and priest. Like that of Christ—King and High Priest. And just as the priests of old were ordained to proclaim the praises of God Most High, the passage makes it clear that we are too. Our purpose here is clearly defined: we were created to declare the praises of the one who called us out of darkness and into his wonderful light! This also refers back to ancient passages:

- . . . my people, my chosen, the people I formed for myself that they may proclaim my praise. (Isa 43:21)

- I will lead the blind by ways they have not known, along unfamiliar paths I will guide them; I will turn the darkness into light before them and make the rough places smooth. These are the things I will do; I will not forsake them. (Isa 42:16)

When we take a moment to reflect on all the ancient passages that Peter references, it is quite amazing!

According to Bible scholar Joel Green, Peter has a definite purpose. Just as the cathedral in Barcelona was under major renovation, so too were the people of God. While the institutions of old still stand, they have been completely made over by God in view of Christ's fulfillment of the law and his role as High Priest and King. His people are also getting a facelift, calling them into their true purpose as proclaimers and revealers of God and his glorious light! In the words of Green, "One might say, then, that Peter has studied the past with an eye to serving the present and especially to showing the continuity between followers of Jesus and Israel of old."[16] While the old sacrificial system is done away with, the purpose and calling of God's chosen people remains unchanged. And that same heritage is passed on to us today.

First, we are still his chosen people, his treasured possession. With our artistic and creative nature comes a certain sensitivity, and with that sensitivity, we often feel less than chosen or treasured. In fact, we often feel excluded, mistreated, and misunderstood. How often have you sat in church, thought of a great, creative idea, and yet had no idea how to make it happen? Or if your congregation would even want or accept it? My mom, who is a wonderful pianist, sat back and wondered why no one ever asked her to play special music for the service. She finally got up the nerve to walk up to the service planner and say, "I've been working on a piece, and was wondering when you'd like me to play it?"

"How about next week?" came the pleasant and instant reply.

We may not always get that easy and encouraging of a reply, but it doesn't mean we give up. Rory Noland's book *The Heart of the Artist* gives both pastor and artist advice on how to close the divide between church and artist. Perhaps you need to buy two copies—one for you and one for your pastor or worship leader.

Second, we are still a royal priesthood, holy nation. We obviously have spent much of this chapter discussing what that means and how you might fit into that.

Are you convinced yet?

Father God, your word speaks clearly to us. We are both chosen and treasured by you. We are to serve as your kingdom of priests, to stand as a holy people, to proclaim your praise among the earth. Lord, help us to walk in these callings. We often don't feel like any of these things are true of us. We don't picture ourselves like you do. Lord, help us know and see. Erase the lies that blind us and hold us back. Give us vision. Give us courage. Help us speak up. Help us support and stand together with the leaders of our churches to proclaim your name. Help us reveal the wonderful light that shines in the darkness. We want to be the church you've called us to be—let the scaffolding and tarps come down!

In the Name of the Master Architect and Builder we pray, amen.

Listen to "Marvelous Light" by Charlie Hall

Digging Deeper:
Getting Our Priestly Praise On

Read: 1 Chronicles 15–16

oday's passage is a long read, but trust me, it's worth it! Did you read *all* of it? If you haven't, read it now and be aware of the many things we've already discussed in this chapter.

And welcome back.

First, let's place this story within its historical context. Many years have passed since God appointed Aaron and his sons as priests. The Israelites have wandered in the desert, later generations have settled in the promised land of Canaan, judges and kings have come and gone. Most recently, King Saul has died, and David has taken his place as king after defeating the Philistines once more. After one failed attempt to bring the Ark of the Covenant back to Jerusalem, David consults the Law of Moses and finds that God has specific requirements set in place. Finally, the ark is brought back *correctly* amidst shouts of joy and the music of rams horns, trumpets, cymbals, lyres, and harps (15:28), and one disdainful look of the soon-to-be-barren Michal, daughter of Saul.

Now that you've read the entire story, were there some things that stood out to you? Several things stand out for me. The priests and Levites are still being set apart, chosen, and consecrated. There is still a hierarchy among the priests and Levites. The law, with its particular attention to details regarding the ark, is still to be followed. And God is still directing his people on how he is to be worshiped. Despite these things remaining the same, there is one stark difference: there is a whole new level of worship!

Under Moses, worship included primarily sacrifices, prayers, intercession, and symbolic action, but little use of the arts in worship. Now, many new instruments, lots of shouting and songs, and even dance are added to the worship of God. Some refer to this as Davidic worship. It is not that songs, shouts, and dance were not used before (see Exod 15), but they were more a part of the informal worship of God. David has brought these elements into the formal worship of God. As we read throughout Chronicles, we find the Israelites bowing, kneeling, laying prostrate, and lifting and clapping their hands.

*The artist in David has brought the artists of his people
into the worship of God!*

Now remember: David is not a descendant of Aaron the high priest. Yet in his position as the king of Israel he serves as a kind of honorary priest before the people of God. Like Melchizedek, he serves as priest and king. Of course, we must also remember that while David makes all the plans to build the temple, God doesn't permit him to build it because of the bloodshed required of him (1 Chr 22:7–8). That honor is passed on to his son Solomon. Also remember: David isn't a Levite, but from the tribe of Judah. Judah's name means "Praise," for as the fourth son of Jacob and Leah, when he was born Leah broke forth in praise. His descendants eventually become the most powerful of all the tribes. (If you'd like to tackle more reading today, see Jacob's blessing of Judah in Gen 49:8–12.)

Just as Judah was blessed, so was David. Just as he was powerful, so was David. And just as Judah brought about praise, so too does King David. This blessing, power, and praise is so much a part of who David was, and he brings this to the psalm of thanksgiving found here in 1 Chronicles 16:8–36. Notice how he calls not just the people but *all of creation* to praise the Lord, the God of Israel:

Praise

Proclaim

Make known

Sing, Tell, Rejoice

Look, Seek, Remember

Sing, Proclaim, Declare

Ascribe, Ascribe to the Lord the glory due his name

Bring an offering, Come before him

Worship the Lord in splendor

Tremble before him, all the earth

Heavens rejoice

Earth be glad

Sea resound

Fields be jubilant

Trees sing for joy

Give thanks

Cry out

Praise

If you haven't figured it out by now, King David is a worshiper! And as the ark is brought to Jerusalem, a new era of worship has begun!

The song of thanksgiving found in 1 Chronicles 16 is a compilation of at least three Psalms: 96, 105, and 106 (none of which are attributed to David, interestingly). It tells the story of God and his people. It is a story of God's covenant, Israel's waywardness, and God's mercy, love, and justice. It calls the people to join creation in praise and adoration of the one whose love endures forever. The final three verses read like a benediction, and the people agree with "Amen" and "Praise the Lord."

As an artist, the worship established by King David should bring you great hope. See how he brings everyone in—this is a participatory kind of worship. There's no sitting back and observing—all of Israel joins in the praise. See how he acknowledges those chosen and designated by name—each and every person is important. See the pictures he paints through his words—the fields are jubilant and trees sing for joy. And look at all the action words!

God still calls us to this kind of praise of him. He wants us to be free, to dance, to shout, to sing. He wants to hear the sound of our instruments, the clang of our cymbals, the blast of our trumpets, the beauty of our strings. He wants us to see creation and be reminded that all of heaven and earth cry out in exultation and jubilation in praise of their Creator.

Lord God, we long to worship you in freedom. We long to bring our gifts openly and unashamedly to you. We have long been held back—by our churches, our leaders, our congregations, *ourselves!* Help us to step out in our priestly calling. Help us to use our music and our mediums to help others praise you—not for our glory, but for yours alone, oh God! We join with the people of Israel who sang to you so long ago and:

> We cry out, "Save us, God our Savior;
> gather us and deliver us from the nations,
> that we may give thanks to your holy name,
> and glory in your praise."
> Praise be to the Lord, the God of Israel,
> from everlasting to everlasting.
> To the God whose love endures forever, amen.

Listen to: "How Great Thou Art" by one of your favorite artists

Digging Deeper:
The Honor of the Priestly Blessing

Read: Numbers 6:22–27

The Aaronic Blessing in today's passage is a familiar one and is still practiced today in many Jewish and Christian churches across the world. It is a prayer that dates back to the earliest years of the Jewish faith, and by the time it is recorded here in Numbers, it was most likely an established part of their worship. In fact, this prayer of blessing was found in burial caves on silver scrolls predating the Dead Sea Scrolls, making it the oldest recorded passage still in existence.[17] When we repeat this prayer today we repeat a prayer that has been spoken for *thousands* of years, through generation after generation of God's people! It is quite remarkable when you stop to think about it.

It is also a beautifully crafted prayer. In Hebrew, the three lines of the prayer consist of an increasing number of words (3, 5, 7), syllables (12, 14, 16) and consonants (15, 20, 25).[18] This intentional pattern communicates a mounting sense of God's expanding graciousness. Like a crescendo in music, it moves us with ever-increasing volume to the final word—*peace*.[19] This is the Hebrew word *shalom*, and it means much more than an absence of strife. From a root word that means perfect or whole, it means health, prosperity, wholeness, well-being, tranquility, serenity, assurance, and perfect balance.[20] *Shalom* is not based on outer circumstances but is the kind of peace that passes understanding. It is not based on material wealth, but a richness of life based on an internal sense of God's abiding presence.

Also notice the frame of this blessing. These are God's instructions to Aaron and sons in their role as priests, and God is very specific in the way he wants his people blessed. In blessing the people, the priests mark them with the name Yahweh, sealing God's ownership and protection over them. And God promises his blessing. Within this frame, it is *Yahweh* that blesses and keeps; *Yahweh* that shines his face upon and is gracious; *Yahweh* that turns his face and gives peace. The blessing doesn't come from the priests—they're simply a conduit of the blessing. The Lord alone is the source of blessing. And not everyone was given the honor of blessing. God blessed Abraham, and he in turn passed God's blessing down through the patriarchs. Here the blessing is passed down through the priests. Blessing was a priestly privilege and was to be spoken with a sense of honor.

The act of blessing is a lost art within the body of believers today. Think about it. When was the last time someone walked up to you and said, "I want to bless you today with God's peace," or when was the last time you did that for someone else? If you are part of a church that does that, consider yourself blessed—*doubly blessed*—because for many of us the only time we bless someone is when they sneeze. In Bible times, blessing meant so much more than we understand today. It was a holy act performed by the patriarchs and priests, and it held great meaning. It wasn't a passing phrase or prayer, but words that spoke life, grace, and peace over the children of God.

Have you ever watched the Changing of the Guard ceremony at the Tomb of the Unknowns at Arlington National Cemetery? We once sat in 100-degree weather watching the guard pace back and forth before the tomb until the relief commander and sentinel appeared. As you watch the changing ritual take place, there is a real sense of honor and reverence. All three turn and salute the tomb, paying respect and tribute to the fallen soldiers who have no name yet represent all the unknown soldiers who died defending our country.

I'm sure you're wondering what this has to do with you as an artist or creative person in the church. In your priestly role, you must understand the honor and privilege you hold. Just as our soldiers have been given a heart of service and courage, you have been given a heart of artistry and creativity. When you approach your canvas, it's as if your commander is passing to you an important honor and responsibility. Just as the commander inspects the sentinel's rifle, the Commander of Heaven inspects your instrument to make sure your music is in tune with the song of heaven. Just as the soldiers face and salute the fallen soldiers, we "face" our congregation and bless them with a "word" from God.

We often don't think of our music, artwork, dramas, videos, photography, and dances as blessings. But God uses these things to speak to his people, to remind them of his blessing over their lives. In your music and song, God blesses and shows his protection of his people. In your paintings, God's face shines upon his people. In your dance, God turns his face towards his people. In your poetry, God brings peace that passes understanding. In your art and creativity, God's places his seal upon his children.

What if next time you stand to sing, play, paint, or perform you picture your Commander in Heaven handing you your "weapon"? Would you approach your task with the knowledge of the honor, responsibility, and privilege that it truly is? What if next time you looked at your "product" as a blessing and not just a song, a picture, or a performance? Would you sing, draw, or perform differently? I challenge you to pray and enter into your role with the mindset of a soldier or priest and see how it changes the gift of blessing you bring.

Commander of the Heavenly Host, help us to see ourselves as your soldiers.
Most High Priest, help us to see ourselves as your priests.
Help us approach every artistic role with honor and holy reverence.
Help us approach every creative act as an opportunity to bless your people.
Help us develop hearts that bless,
hands that bless,
lives that bless.
Thank you that your face shines upon us all.
Help us reflect you more brightly.
In the Name of the God who blesses his children, amen.

Listen to: "The Lord Bless You and Keep You" by John Rutter, or find a recording of the Aaronic Blessing sung in Hebrew, its original language

Digging Deeper:
Standing in the Gap

Read: Numbers 16

No greater picture exists in the Bible of the intercessory role of the priest than this one, and it points directly to the intercessory role of Christ as our mediator in heaven. Imagine the scene. Envision each heightening moment in the drama: God's presence hanging like a cloud over the tabernacle; people wrongfully casting blame, causing God's wrath to rise against his people; Moses and Aaron falling on their faces before God; Moses yelling instructions to Aaron, and Aaron scrambling to follow even as the plague begins to spread among the people.

The plague sweeps across the camp, people dropping in its path (if you need help, picture the Army of the Dead sweeping across Pelennor Fields in the final battle scene in *The Lord of the Rings: The Return of the King* movie). Then, amidst the death and destruction, Aaron rises and stands in the gap—literally between the living and the dead. He walks right up to the enemy line, putting himself directly in harm's way to protect the people against the advancing plague, armed with only a censor containing incense from God's holy altar.

And what happens? The plague stops. As quickly as it descended, it dissipates. If the exodus of God's people is a drama, then this is one of the most intense scenes.

Let's place this drama in its context. The Israelite nation has traveled up from Egypt and now find themselves in a holding pattern for doubting God's provision as they stood before the Promised Land. In Numbers 14 they start to grumble, "Wouldn't we be better off if we'd have stayed in Egypt?" Except for Joshua and Caleb, God curses them all to forty years of wanderings in the desert. Here in chapter 16, we find the people grumbling yet again and blaming Moses and Aaron that they weren't able to enter the land of milk and honey! Oh, won't they ever learn?

A group of leaders within the community rises up against Moses and Aaron, and the anger of the Lord boils up against them. In the ensuing drama, we find Moses and Aaron on their faces before God *three times* (16:4, 22, 45). They understand God's holiness, wrath, and justice and have learned that the safest place is down on their faces in reverence before God.

One can assume that lying there prostrate before God, they cry out to him, interceding on behalf of this unruly nation. Interestingly, back in Numbers 12, we find Aaron and their sister Miriam grumbling about Moses behind his back. When God calls them out on it, he strikes Miriam with leprosy. Scripture tells us that Moses intercedes for Miriam: "So Moses cried out to the Lord, 'Please, God, heal her!' (12:13)," and God heals her.

So Moses and Aaron understand what it means to intercede, to stand in the gap, in their priestly roles. Yet in the passage above, it is interesting to note the gap Aaron is standing in. He is literally standing *between the living and the dead*. In this way, he foreshadows the work of our Savior, Jesus Christ who would stand between us, the living, and our sin, which like a plague includes the death we surely deserved. Aaron offers up incense, which represents sacrifice, worship, a fragrant offering to God. It has also been used to illustrate our prayers (Ps 141:2; Rev 5:8; 8:3–4). Christ also offers his life as a sacrifice in worship, an offering to God. The book of Hebrews also tells us that Christ lives to make intercession for his people and that he stands as a mediator of the new covenant between God and man.

I love what Bible scholar David Stubbs says about Aaron in this passage:

> Aaron now shows his priestly zeal in a more visible way. Just as some kind of "plague" breaks out from God as an extension of his wrath, Aaron apparently steps into its path, standing "between the dead and the living," risking himself while praying and censing to God in order to keep the plague from advancing. In doing so, he shows great love for the people he is priest to. Just as the sweet smell of incense is pleasing to God, so too is that which the incense symbolizes: Aaron's zeal and prayers of intercession for the people. Aaron's actions atone for the people's sins because they are worthy tokens of the dedication and service God desires of all his priestly people. . . . Aaron's action with the censor both atones for the sin of the people and provides a wonderful symbol of the calling of priestly leaders.[21]

Aaron's actions have Christ written all over them! And in the same way that Christ serves as High Priest, as his hands and feet and as a holy priesthood, we too are called into this same kind of service.

When was the last time you thought of your artwork, medium, instrument, words, or movements like a censor? For most of us, that answer would be never. In fact, I've never thought of mine in that way. While I have long understood my worship as intercession, I've never thought of it as a censor filled with incense. Censors and the incense they hold symbolize the aroma of worship, sacrifice, prayers, and zealous intercession. What if we, as artists and creative Christians, began to picture our worship in this way?

Can you imagine the power and impact it would have?
> If Aaron's censor could dispel a deathly plague,
>> then how much more could our own worship?
>>> What if we took our priestly role more seriously?
>>> What if we loved the people we serve as Aaron did?
>> What if we approached our artistry and creativity with zeal for the Lord?

Next time you help lead worship, act in a drama, dance in church, or paint for a service, can you picture Aaron's censor? Perhaps you could prepare by praying facedown before the Lord like Moses and Aaron. Perhaps you could picture the enemy or sin in the room advancing like a plague. Perhaps you could visualize yourself walking among the people with your medium as a censor of incense. Perhaps you can see your act of worship standing in the gap bringing life where there is death. What would happen if we could imagine just for a second that God could work in this way through our art forms and mediums?

Father of our imagination, today we have spent our time picturing, visualizing, and envisioning. We need your help to see for the way gets so cloudy sometimes. We lose track of our purpose, our calling, our vocation. We neglect to see the pictures you have painted in your word. It's as if we spend most of our lives walking through an art exhibit with blinders on, failing to see all the images you have created for us. Help us see earth with heavenly eyesight.

And Lord Jesus, help us to picture ourselves walking beside you with our censors of worship. When we're unsure help us remember to serve you with zeal, sacrifice, and love for the people we serve. We thank you and praise you that you stood between the living and the dead, filling in the gap and bringing us eternal life. We fall facedown before you for you alone deserve all the honor, reverence, and glory.

In the Name of he who stood in the gap, Jesus, amen.

Listen to: "Facedown" by Matt Redman

Digging Deeper:
Wise Counsel to Kings

Read: Matthew 2:1–12

ust this morning I read an article about the discovery of a shard of clay that mentions the town of Bethlehem.[22] The interesting (and most important) thing about this discovery is that up until now there has been no archeological find that supported the existence of the ancient town of Bethlehem. Of course, if you grew up in church, you never doubted the existence of the town of Bethlehem—after all, it was where baby Jesus was born. But outside the safety of our four walls, there were many "experts" who doubted both its existence and, moreover, the Bible's historical accuracy because of it. It goes to show that just because you can't prove something doesn't mean it isn't real or true. There is so much more to discover. We need to keep digging!

Nearly every year at Christmas, we read the story above of the visit of the wise men. We hear about how they sought him, the gifts they brought, their dreams, and their diverted trip home. But what can we discover if we keep digging? I want you to turn your attention to verse 4: "When [Herod] had called together all the people's chief priests and teachers of the law, he asked them where the Messiah was to be born." What can we unearth if we mine deeper here?

First, note that King Herod is digging too—digging for information. He's heard some disturbing news and has called together all of the chief priests and teachers of the law to uncover the truth. The chief priests are the folks we've been studying about here in this chapter. Remember that one of their roles was to help the Jewish people interpret their scriptures. The teachers of the law, or scribes as they are often called, were also experts in the ancient scriptures and Mosaic Law.

Now these two groups don't really get along. As with any group of experts, the membership has become somewhat political, and here in this story King Herod is pitting them against one another. One priest or scribe could've answered his question, but the king calls them all together so no one would trick him. He's counting on their disagreements to keep them both honest.

As we continue to excavate this passage, do you notice the role of the priests? They are called to offer wisdom and guidance to the king and royal court. They have an audience with the king! This is different than when God first established the priesthood, because at that time there was no king. However, remember that Moses and Aaron worked together in leading the people of Israel, and this leadership role has carried over into later the generations of monarchs and kings. Throughout history, kings have often called on spiritual leaders for guidance and wisdom. We see this happen even yet today. These leaders are counting not just on their expertise in all things spiritual, but also on their wisdom, their ability to sit back and observe a situation from a different angle.

As creative visionaries in the church, we too can offer guidance, wisdom, and a different viewpoint to our leaders. They may call on us to do so, as in the story above, or they may not. But it is a role of the priest and the artist, and we must be good stewards of this responsibility. We can't flippantly tell our leaders, "You should do this" or "God told me that." And we can't always control what our leaders will do with the information we give them, but it is our role to give it nonetheless. Once the information is given, we humbly walk away and allow God to move in them to make the final decision.

Furthermore, the wisdom we offer is not just for our leaders, but also for our entire congregations. People often look to our artistic offerings for wisdom and insight. Most of us can think of a song that helped us see things differently, more deeply, just by listening. The writer of Psalm 49 understands this responsibility: "Hear this, all peoples! Give ear, all inhabitants of the world. . . . My mouth shall speak wisdom; the meditation of my heart shall be understanding. I will incline my ear to a proverb; I will solve my riddle to the music of the lyre" (vv. 1, 3–4, ESV). As a harpist inclines her ear towards the strings of her instrument to hear more clearly, the writer here has inclined his ear to a proverb, a saying, a question. He has spent time pondering and is singing his observations to the music of his instrument. Sounds like a worship leader to me!

We cannot approach this role with pride, arrogance, laziness, or negligence.

We must act with a deep sense of the weight of responsibility we hold.

This is an honor and responsibility that cannot be taken lightly.

Notice the priests and scribes in Matthew 2 passage are not speaking out of their own thoughts—they are quoting Scripture. God's word guides them in their speech. They're not giving their own opinion—they're speaking out of a deep knowledge of the law and scriptures.

This is one of the purposes of these devotional Bible studies you are reading and studying along with me. We must learn to dig deeper into the word of God. We can't just skim the surface and expect to have spiritual knowledge of any depth or clarity. Like archeologists, we must excavate and sift through the dirt to find the treasures of God's word. There is so much to be mined from his word. Search the Internet or the library for Bible commentaries to learn more about a passage. Don't read just one, for that is only one person's opinion. Read many and gather different viewpoints to understand.

Then, the next time you're called on to give your opinion or wisdom on a matter, whether its through words or through an art form, speak out of that base of knowledge. It's so easy for us to state our own opinions and speak out of our own knowledge or experience. It is much harder to stop and consider what God's word might say and then form our opinions based on a biblical understanding.

Father God, you are the burier of deep and hidden treasures. Help me Lord. Next time I am asked to give counsel to my leaders, to help lead worship or offer my artistic gift to service, help me dig out your word, mine from your wisdom, and unearth what you would have me say. Through prayer and careful consideration, I will excavate the many treasures you have buried for my discovery. I will incline my ear to hear your melody, your harmonies. Thank you for entrusting me with this responsibility. Help me to approach it with humility and diligence. Allow the meditation of my heart to bring understanding, wisdom, and guidance.

In the mysterious Name of El Elyon, the Most High God, I pray, amen.

Listen to: "The More I Seek You" by Zach Neese

Endnotes

1. It might be helpful to read Heb 4:14—5:10 and 7:1—8:13. These passages, which read much like Jewish midrash, serve to connect Christ to Melchizedek and explain why Christ is qualified to serve as our High Priest in heaven. As artists and creative Christians, this information aids us in understanding our priestly role in the church. Also, for more thorough research see Lane, *Hebrews 1–8*.

2. Lane, *Hebrews 1–8*, 123.

3. Ibid., 162.

4. Nouwen, *Wounded Healer*, 75. I consider this book a must-read for anyone in Christian leadership and ministry.

5. Begbie, *Voicing Creation's Praise*, 181.

6. Ibid., 209.

7. Nouwen, *Wounded Healer*, 76.

8. Best, *Unceasing Worship*. This is another must-read for the artist and creative Christian. Best has a very biblical and holistic approach to worship and the creative arts.

9. Idid., 112.

10. Ibid., 159.

11. L'Engle, *Walking*, 127.

12. Best, *Unceasing Worship*, 116.

13. Ibid., 127.

14. Begbie, *Voicing Creation's Praise*, 227.

15. L'Engle, *Walking*, 196–97.

16. Green, *I Peter*, 63.

17. Olson, *Numbers*, 41.

18. Brown, *Message of Numbers*, 55.

19. Stubbs, *Numbers*, 74.

20. Brown, *Message of Numbers*, 59.

21. Stubbs, *Numbers*, 148.

22. Friedman, "Ancient Shard."

five

Give Me a Sign:
Symbolic Action & the Artist as Prophet

*"I have appealed to you through parables
acted out by the prophets."*

ONCE SHARED A bus ride with the dance company from Gallaudet University. All over the bus, they were deeply and actively engrossed in many conversations. Excitement and joy filled the air as they discussed the performance that had just amazed me beyond words. Amidst these conversations, I simply sat and watched for I couldn't hear a word they said. You see the dancers of Gallaudet are deaf and hearing impaired. They speak through hand motions commonly referred to as American Sign Language. They understood each other perfectly; I only understood their excitement and joy. And they dance with the same exuberance. They have found an art form and a language that coincide and speak volumes to their audiences.

Art Speaks

The arts have long been used as a way to communicate to others. An artist spends many hours creating an image that "speaks" to its viewers. Sometimes we "hear" what the artist is saying. Other times we "hear" another message that the artist may not have originally intended—yet it speaks nonetheless. Each of the arts "speaks" in a different way: visual arts through form, color, line; cinematic and photographic arts through angle, lighting, scene, musical score; dramatic arts through voice, inflection, character, scenery; dance through movement, line, contraction, release; song through rhythm, volume, lyrics (or lack of), instrumentation; poetry and the written arts through word, meter, rhyme, climax, foreshadowing. I'm sure you can add many more "voices" you might employ as you speak through artistic expression.

Art functions as a type of language. As a language, it relies on symbols and symbolism. Aristotle once said, "A soul never thinks without a picture." When we think, process, and attempt to understand, we do so through symbols. The letter *A* represents certain sounds, but it also represents a good grade, the top of the pack (A-list), or a single unit of something (*a* dog vs. three dogs). We attach meaning to the things we see, read, and experience. These meanings point to the symbolic nature of our language, both spoken and unspoken, as we attempt to communicate with others in the world around us.

Dancer and author Celeste Snowber Schroeder uses the term "movement metaphor" to describe the symbolic nature of movement. She states:

> Our gestures, postures, expression, and creative movement can all be 'movement metaphors,' ways of communicating something else through the power of body language. Bowed heads, reaching arms, jumping feet, closed or open bodies all become movement metaphors that reveal a deeper reality. Metaphors through words create a visual image in our imaginations. Translating those metaphors in our bodies fleshes out that image so we can see it and experience it in our bones.[1]

In dance, we also add to this the "language" of the music. Music communicates through lyrics and the music itself—the way it rises and falls, swells and fades away, echoes with a single instrument or bellows with a full orchestra. The combination of all three (movement, lyrics, and music) communicates at a depth impossible for any of the three standing alone.

Symbolism in Art & Religion

Symbols, in essence, connect one thing to another. Margaret Fisk Taylor was one of the pioneers in bringing worship dance back into the church in the 1960s and 1970s. In her book *A Time to Dance*, she discusses the meaning and uses of symbols: "The term symbol means basically 'to bring together.' The function of a symbol is (1) to bring together various relationships into a simple whole, (2) to make something more meaningful through this relationship, and (3) to gather significance for members of a group so that they understand what the symbol represents."[2] And she goes on to make this powerful statement:

No area of communication is more dependent
on symbolic expression than is religious experience.

Thomas Kane confirms this: "Art, ritual, and dance can elevate and expand our spiritual horizons. Symbols can express what the heart feels and our tongue cannot articulate. There is a ritual world of symbols and dance."[3] And Jeremy Begbie adds, "In the mission and witness of the Church, the arts will be no mere decorative luxury: as any experienced Christian communicator will know, the outside will frequently be grasped by the truth of the gospel more profoundly if it is embodied in artistic form than if it is couched in straightforward prose."[4] Symbolic and artistic expression and movement allows us to *see the unseen*, to somehow break through the boundary between earth and heaven and see God—even if it is only as in a mirror dimly (1 Cor 13:12). Carla DeSola, another pioneer in the worship dance movement, agrees: "I think of dance, and all the arts, as bridges between the visible and the invisible world of the spirit," says DeSola.[5]

Bob Rognlien has written a book called *Experiential Worship: Encountering God with Heart, Soul, Mind, and Strength*. I highly recommend this book for anyone serving a church in a creative arts or worship ministry. He speaks of the importance of the arts as a means to help people connect with their emotions in worship because "they speak the language of the soul." He continues: "In God-given artistic expression, reflections of divine beauty become an opening for truth to penetrate the deepest part of a human being and bring transformation."[6] He goes on to quote author Ken Gire from *Windows of the Soul*:

> God gave us art, music, sculpture, drama, and literature. He gave them as footpaths to lead us out of our hiding places and as signposts to lead us along in our search for what was lost. . . . We reach for God in many ways. Through our sculptures and our Scriptures. Through our pictures and our prayers. Through our writing and our worship. And through them he reaches for us. . . . When we look long enough at a scene from a movie, a page from a book, a person from across the room, and when we look deeply enough, these moments framed in our minds grow transparent. Everywhere we look, there are pictures that are not really pictures but windows. If only we have eyes to see beyond the paint. If we look

closely we can see something beyond the two dimensions within the frame, something beyond the ordinary colors brushed across the canvas of our everyday lives.[7]

Yes! If we only have eyes to see beyond.

The creative arts used in worship paint an image that speaks to its viewer—whether that "viewer" is a congregation, an audience of curious seekers, or God himself. You see, sacred art communicates in two ways:

1. It speaks the heart of the worshiper to the God he or she serves. As the artist worships through his or her art form, he or she is able to express his or her heart of adoration and praise to the Father. In this role, the artist acts as *priest*, standing as an advocate between God and his people. We discussed our priestly role as an artist in the previous chapter.

2. It speaks the heart of God to his people. The arts have the power of bypassing the mind and going directly to the heart. God uses his artists to speak his heart, so that his people are able to see and hear the truth of his desperate love towards them. In this role, the artist acts as *prophet*, speaking the voice of God through his or her art form or medium.

Symbolic Action of the Prophets

In Scripture we often see the prophet communicating his message through actions. These are called symbolic acts, sign acts, or mimed prophecies. The prophets Jeremiah, Ezekiel, and Hosea are most commonly referred to in the study of symbolic action, but it was used by many prophets (See the Appendix for a complete list). Symbolic acts follow a basic form: the prophet is given a command to do something specific; the prophet carries out the command; an interpretation is given either by the prophet or, most often, by God speaking through the prophet.[8] It was a *visual symbol* that was always accompanied by the *spoken word*. The symbolic actions of the prophets reveal that it is a *combination of the spoken and the visual* that allows the audience to hear and see—to experience the message through two senses instead of just one.

As God instructs the prophet to uses action to illustrate his message, it helps the receiver of that message to see as well as hear. God shows tiny glimpses of himself to his people! God says to us: "I have also spoken to [you by] the prophets, and I have multiplied visions [for you] and [have appealed to you] through parables acted out by the prophets" (Hos 12:10, AMP). He wants us to see, to know, to understand. In his final instructions to the disciples, we find this conversation between Christ and Philip:

> Jesus said, "I am the Road, also the Truth, also the Life. No one gets to the Father apart from me. If you really knew me, you would know my Father as well. From now on, you do know him. You've even seen him!"
>
> Philip said, "Master, show us the Father; then we'll be content."
>
> "You've been with me all this time, Philip, and you still don't understand? To see me is to see the Father. So how can you ask, 'Where is the Father?' Don't you believe that I am in the Father and the Father is in me? The words that I speak to you aren't mere words. I don't just make them up on my own. The Father who resides in me crafts each word into a divine act." (John 14:6–10, TM)

In this way, Christ is revealed as the greatest of all prophets and the greatest of all symbolic acts. The prophet, Jesus Christ, speaks on behalf of God the Father. And his words are living words, each crafted by the hand of God into a "divine act." To see and hear Christ is to see and hear God.

In his book *Prophecy in Ancient Israel*, author J. Lindblom tells us that the phrase "symbolic action" does not go far enough. In fact, he says,

> It is nearer the truth to say that such an action is a form of the divine word. It is *verbum visible*, a visible word, and shares in all the qualities which distinguish the divine word . . . An important feature [of the divine word] was the effective power of this word. As a divine word, the word uttered by a prophet had an effective power. The same is true of the visible word, the so-called symbolic action. Such an action served not only to represent and make evident a particular fact, but also to make this fact a reality.[9]

Scholar and author Joseph Blenkinsopp points out that these symbolic acts are more than illustrative "visual aids" for the prophet: "Their purpose was to enhance the force of the spoken word, to make possible the more intense kind of identification with it that successful theater can achieve."[10] In this regard, it is similar to the actor who becomes fully involved with their character. The prophet Hosea is a perfect example. As we will see, his life was taken over by the symbolic acts he was to "perform" for the sake of Yahweh's message to his people. When was the last time you thought of your art as a visible word that had the power of the divine word? That is quite an honor *and* a responsibility.

Everybody and Every Body

You might argue that the audience does not really participate in the symbolic expression of the artist. Refer back to Taylor's description of symbols. Her third point demonstrates how the performer and audience both participate as a community in defining the meaning of the symbol itself. In order for a symbol to be a symbol, there must be shared understanding of the meaning. Think of the use of gestures. Some gestures are universal in nature; other gestures will cause offense in one culture, but not in another; some gestures must be described in order to be understood.

There is also a vicarious nature to the arts—one where the viewers become not just emotionally, but also physically involved as they observe. Schroeder writes about the vicarious nature of the dance, stating: "Even though the worshiper may be sitting in a pew or chair, he or she can kinesthetically be taken through the psalmist's words as the dancer's limbs extend the meaning in her/his body. The congregation can physically and spiritually be drawn into God's presence as the word of God is incarnated in dance."[11] Just as the Word became flesh and dwelt among us, so the spoken word becomes physical flesh and dwells here with us, and we see the glory of God in human form.

As the dancer moves, she allows the congregation to move along with her. In their minds, they too take flight. Their bodies, contained in a pew for far too long, are released to experience the sensation of movement. If they allow themselves, they too will find their muscles tightening and releasing, stretching and contracting, reaching and pulling back. This vicarious nature is true of all art forms. We become wrapped up in characters. We paint huge brushstrokes in our own minds. We ourselves spin and are molded as the pot is thrown.

We must understand that humans are created as whole beings—mind, body, and spirit; heart, soul, mind, and strength. Platonic thinking has invaded our Western culture, separating our mind, body, and soul. Symbolic movement calls us back to a holistic, Hebraic mindset that sees the person as one—just as God is One. The Trinity is a perfect example of a holistic nature. Three persons, yet one. Separate functions working together in complete unity. Father, Son, and Holy Spirit—One God. If we apply that

Trinitarian concept to our human form, we find the mind, body, and soul working together—different functions, working together in unity. If a person becomes paralyzed, do they no longer function as a whole? No! The mind contributes greater self-determination. The soul contributes greater courage. The body continues to move with help from the entire being.

As people we realize that sometimes words just aren't enough. As a dancer, actress, singer, and artist, I have come to realize that my body and its related movement are vital to my ability to communicate. There are times when my words fail me, where my words fall short of the worship I long to express to my God. The same holds true as I seek to communicate God's message of grace, hope, and love to others. Words alone do not suffice to explain the glory of God and his abundant, transforming love for his children. Psalm 103:1 (NLT) says: "Let all that I am praise the LORD; with my whole heart, I will praise his holy name." Let all that I am—not just my mind, not just my body, not just my soul, but *all that I am*—praise the Lord!

Digging Deeper into Symbolic Action

We do not create art purely for art's sake, but for God's sake. Through our creativity, artwork, songs, and movements, we speak God's glory, and we speak it back to him. This is our priestly role. We also create for the sake of others, so that they may be blessed by him speaking to his people. This is our prophetic role. Just as the prophets were obedient in acting out and speaking out their message of repentance and God's faithfulness, so too must we. We must take very seriously our given task to communicate God's truth through the arts. We are a prophetic voice, and every "word" we "speak" through our God-given creativity can be a word that speaks to the lives of those who "hear" it as we create. As we study the prophets and their symbolic acts, may we be reminded of our own role as a Christian artist called to speak through our art to God's people.

Digging Deeper: Symbolic Action & the Artist as Prophet

Hosea 1 & 3: Oh Love That Will Not Let Me Go
Jeremiah 13: Rightful Pride & Thankful Praise
Jeremiah 32: The Dance of Travail
Ezekiel 21:6–7: The Pain of the Prophetic Artist
Ezekiel 4:4–17: The Turning of the Face

A complete list of the symbolic acts of the prophets is found in the Appendix.

Digging Deeper:
Oh Love That Will Not Let Me Go

Read: Hosea 1:2–3 & 3:1–5

The prophet Hosea writes as one who has experienced grief. It is this grief that allows him to speak the very anguish of God. As we see from the passages above, God asked Hosea to take an adulteress wife—a prostitute who is far from worthy enough to be married to a prophet of God. He obeys, and his obedience will lead him to a life of anguish as he watches his wife cheat on him and return to her life of prostitution. Hosea's actions symbolize God's love for his people, as well as the punishment that is due the nation of Israel in forsaking her first love. Gomer's actions and disobedience symbolize Israel's adultery.

The book of Hosea is overflowing with poetic language—at once very fierce and, yet, very tender and loving. In one respect, Hosea's writing is violent—often drenched in images of sexual sin, molestation, and wicked idolatry. We see a God that will break the nation of Israel because of her unfaithfulness. He will place a heavy "yoke on her fair neck" so that she can "break up the unplowed ground" (10:11–12). In another respect, God speaks lovingly to his wayward bride, "betrothing [her] to [him] forever . . . in righteousness and justice" (3:19). It is as if God himself is wrestling with the full range of emotions within him: "How can I give you up? . . . My heart is changed within me; all my compassion is aroused" (11:8).

And, the truth is, God can't give us up. He loves us beyond our capacity to ever deserve it. He loves us with a jealous, redeeming, conquering, unfailing love—a love that knows no limits! And like Gomer, he comes and redeems us

even when we run away
even when we return to our former ways of sin and rebellion.

Just as Hosea put restrictions on Gomer, so too may God in order to protect us and to encourage us to seek hard after him. We hear his voice say: "Because she has been unfaithful to me, I will allure her into the wilderness where I will speak tenderly to her. There I will make her place of trouble, a door of hope" (2:14–15, paraphrase).

Where have you struggled?

What areas of sin cause you trouble?

What things tempt you to return to former ways of rebellion?

It is in those places, where God wants to meet you. He wants to meet you there and show you a door of hope—a hope that rests in his redeeming love. Read Romans 5:6–10.

Reflect on God's great love

a love that sends his son as an atoning sacrifice for our sins

even while we were yet sinners!

Give him your sin, your struggle, your trouble.

Turn it over to him.

He is there to redeem you, to buy you back.
Because you're worth it to him!

As you return to him, ask him if there's anything he wants to "restrict." Perhaps there's an issue that holds you back, and God wants to limit that in order to show you the full extent of his love and the full extent of your potential as you live in communion with him. Give it all to him in anticipation and excitement as you seek to do his will.

As we end this study, I am reminded of the hymn "Oh Love That Will Not Let Me Go," written by George Matheson. In his own words, he reveals that it was created out of a place of struggle and conflict within him:

> My hymn was composed in the manse of Innelan [Argyleshire, Scotland] on the evening of the 6th of June, 1882, when I was 40 years of age. I was alone in the manse at that time. It was the night of my sister's marriage, and the rest of the family were staying overnight in Glasgow. Something happened to me, which was known only to myself, and which caused me the most severe mental suffering. The hymn was the fruit of that suffering. It was the quickest bit of work I ever did in my life. I had the impression of having it dictated to me by some inward voice rather than of working it out myself. I am quite sure that the whole work was completed in five minutes, and equally sure that it never received at my hands any retouching or correction. I have no natural gift of rhythm. All the other verses I have ever written are manufactured articles; this came like a dayspring from on high.[12]

The hymn speaks of humanity's struggle and of God's unrelenting love. Let it be our prayer.

O Love that will not let me go,
I rest my weary soul in thee;
I give thee back the life I owe,
That in thine ocean depths its flow
May richer, fuller be.

O Joy that seekest me through pain,
I cannot close my heart to thee;
I trace the rainbow through the rain,
And feel the promise is not vain,
That morn shall tearless be.

O Cross that liftest up my head,
I dare not ask to fly from thee;
I lay in dust life's glory dead,
And from the ground there blossoms red
Life that shall endless be.

In your loving Name we pray, amen.

Listen to: "O Love That Will Not Let Me Go" by Dave Hunt

Digging Deeper:
Rightful Pride & Thankful Praise

Read: Jeremiah 13:1–11

In this symbolic act, Jeremiah the prophet is asked to perform several actions before he is ever told their meaning or significance. However, Jeremiah doesn't need a reason—he simply obeys. We must also walk in this kind of obedience to God. Sometimes God asks me to do something that at the time seems odd or weird or, frankly, makes me feel very uncomfortable. This is especially true when we create. Sometimes in the midst of our rehearsals, studio time, or editing, we sense God nudging us to do something that doesn't make sense. I find when I listen to his voice, he blesses that obedience, and in the end, his changes make sense, and I understand why he asked me to do what seemed unclear, strange, or uncomfortable. This is an important lesson we take from this passage. However, I want to focus on a less obvious lesson.

The exact meaning of the word translated here as "linen belt" is unclear. It has also been translated *girdle, waistcloth,* and *loincloth.*[13] Despite this ambiguity, two things are clear: it is a garment worn close to the body, and it is made of linen, a "pure" fabric worn by priests. By instructing him to "not let it touch water," God is further enforcing the need for this garment to be unspoiled before being worn. After wearing this garment, he is instructed to hide it in a crevice in the rocks where it remains until he is later instructed to retrieve it. By then, however, the garment is ruined. Scholar J. A. Thompson explains: "Just as the linen girdle had been spoiled, so also would the gross pride of Judah and . . . Jerusalem be destroyed. The girdle represented the people of God, pure and untarnished at the time of their call (Jer. 2:2–3). As the girdle clings to a man's waist, so the entire house of Israel and . . . Judah once clung to Yahweh that they might be his people, his source of renown and praise and glory."[14] A thing that was once pure and blameless before the Lord has become tainted with pride and rebellion. And Judah will pay for this in its destruction.

How does this apply to us as artists? Take a moment to think about the things you are proud of—the things that fill you with rejoicing and blessing. Your family, spouse, children? Your friends? Your church? Your ministry? Your creativity? Your accomplishments? Your spirituality? Now, these things are all good things. Things we should be proud of. Places where we should find blessing and be filled with rejoicing. But we must also be cautious. Those very things, like Judah, can also be the source of our downfall. Pride in and of itself is not a bad thing, but it can so easily become tainted with a sense of self-accomplishment and self-importance. Our pride must always be kept in check with a sense of humility and the knowledge that all these blessings come from the hand of the Father and should never be taken for granted. We cannot become puffed up with our own sense of arrogance. Humility is the key!

Read Ephesians 1:3–23. The apostle Paul enforces that we are holy and blameless before the Lord—just like God's chosen people of Israel. As you keep reading you see that there is much to be proud of, to find blessing in, to rejoice in:

> You are adopted as his sons and daughters through Jesus Christ!
> He lavishes his grace upon you, with wisdom and understanding!
> *You are chosen and marked with a seal of the Holy Spirit!*

You have much to be proud of! Notice Paul's pride in this church in Ephesus. And then notice how the rest of the chapter is given over to the praise of God. Paul's pride is deeply rooted in the acknowledgment that it is all *from* God and *for* his glory and praise. Then, on top of all that, he prays that God will give them even more blessings!

God is the source of all our blessings. Take a moment to "count your blessings." As you do, give praise to the Lord. Create something as an act of praise. Get on your feet and dance a dance of praise for all he has done. Paint and with every brush stroke declare his glory and beauty. Grab your camera and photograph all the things you consider blessings. Praise God for his faithfulness in your life, in your ministry, and in your art.

> *Praise God from whom all blessings flow!*
> *Praise Him all creatures here below!*
> *Praise Him above ye heavenly hosts!*
> *Praise Father, Son and Holy Ghost!*
> *Amen.*[15]

Listen to: "Bless His Name" by Tony Sanchez (Vineyard Music)

Digging Deeper:
The Dance of Travail

Read: Jeremiah 32

In the midst of the siege of the city of Jerusalem, while Jeremiah is sitting in jail, God commands him to buy a piece of property from his cousin. Now God has asked Jeremiah to buy things before—a linen belt in 13:1 and pottery in 19:1—and both of those items were destroyed. Now, God wants him to buy land that will soon be taken by the Chaldeans. As always, Jeremiah is obedient. And only after the deed is finalized, does he pray for understanding: "Nothing is too hard for you" (32:17b, ESV) . . . "yet you have told me to buy this land when it will belong to the Chaldeans" (32:25, paraphrase). God confirms Jeremiah's statement in verse 27:

"Is anything too hard for me?"

In the end, God explains the prophetic promise that is embedded in Jeremiah's actions: the land of God's people will be restored.

In her book *Dancing into the Anointing*, Aimee Verduzco Kovacs discusses the Dance of Travail, which is "a dance of faith where we thank God for the answer to our prayer before the answer is visible. In this dance we proclaim to the principalities of darkness that our God is able to do above and beyond what we ask of him . . . [It is] a victory dance by faith."[16] When a dancer moves in obedience in the midst of difficulty, he dances the dance of travail. Just like Jeremiah, in our obedience, we speak words of honor and praise despite our situation.

A woman giving birth is another example of travail. As she pushes with every ounce of strength, she is using her body in a kind of dance of travail. Jesus tells us this: "A woman giving birth to a child has pain because her time has come; but when her baby is born she forgets the anguish because of her joy that a child is born into the world" (John 16:21). She endures the pain because there is promise at the end of her travail. As the baby finally emerges and is placed upon her belly, she witnesses that promise—in the flesh! Her travail has resulted in a promise revealed. As that baby grows, she continues to travail—from the terrible twos through the tempestuous teenage years—laying a sure foundation. And someday if that child rebels like the prodigal, she continues to travail. Her promise rests in the foundation that has been laid in this child's life, and although she may travail for many years as she watches that child turn from the truth of God, she dances in the promise of the return of the prodigal. And just as the father watched and waited, she watches, waiting to see her child returning even from a long way off.

So, where in your life do things look bleak?

Where are you praying like Jeremiah for understanding?

Where are you in the midst of labor pains in your ministry?

Perhaps those are the very areas where God wants you

to dance the dance of travail.

There's an often-quoted saying that states:

"Hope is hearing the melody of the future.

Faith is to dance to it now."[17]

Do you have the faith to dance to the melody of the future? Can you dance as though the future is now even when your present circumstances say otherwise? Those are the places of real faith building. Are you willing?

Not a dancer, you say? Then create as if dancing the dance of travail. Pick up that project that has alluded you—you know, the one that you've never quite finished—and press in! Be determined to finish it. Keep painting. Keep weaving. Keep pressing the shutter. Keep writing. Keep working on that script. Keep putting notes and chords together. And as you press in, consider it your own personal dance of travail. And as you create, press into God. Create as if the answers to your prayers lie in the act of creating. Create as an act of worship and praise. Do not give up! Press in! Travail!

Did you notice the passage in Jeremiah is a passage filled with promise? Notice Jeremiah's prayer in 32:16–25. He *first* declares the mighty power of God; he *begins* with praise. Next he remembers God's faithfulness through many generations. He calls to memory God's acts of kindness. Then, and only then, does he ask the question, "Why?"

Spend some time praising God and remembering what he has done in your life. As you call these things to mind, speak them out, thanking and praising God for his faithfulness. Then ask the Lord for understanding where there is confusion in your life or ministry. And then, until he answers, dance the dance of travail. Dance in the memories of all he has done. Dance in the promises of his great faithfulness to you.

Lord, I pray that as your artists press in, you will hear their prayers. That you will hear every brush stroke as a prayer of their heart; that you will see their "rolls" of film as an endless prayer of hope and praise; that every word they write will be words that bring life, promise, and mercy even in the midst of their own pain and travail. As they literally press into the clay in front of them, that you will see them spiritually pressing in to you. I pray that their art will prophetically speak your heart; that their creations will be a source of your love to others. I pray that in their travail you will bless them with specific answers to the prayers that they have laid before your throne.

I pray these things in the Name of he who persevered until his victory was won, in the Name of Jesus Christ.

Amen.

Listen to: "Be Near" by Shane & Shane

Digging Deeper:
The Pain of the Prophetic Artist

Read: Ezekiel 21:6–7

zekiel was quite the dramatist. His prophecies were laden with symbolic acts. This is "Act 1" in a two-act play that foretells the fall of Jerusalem under the sword of Nebuchadnezzar. Yahweh begins by telling Ezekiel to groan before the people—and he is to groan in such a way to draw attention so that they question why he is acting this way. This is a deep groaning—a sighing that comes from the depths of his being (literally his "loins"[18]). But he isn't just acting here. He is feeling deep emotional pain that is attached to his role as prophet. There is a sense of an "intense emotional identification"[19] with the people of Judah. These are Ezekiel's people, his own nation. Their fate is Ezekiel's fate.

If we are creating in true prophetic fashion, then the same should be true of us as an artistic revealer of God's voice of truth. In his book *The Living Reminder*, Henri Nouwen observes how the minister is called to a connective and collective grief:

> The great vocation of the minister is to continuously make connections between the human story and the divine story. We have inherited a story which needs to be told in such a way that the many painful wounds about which we hear day after day can be liberated from their isolation and be revealed as part of God's relationship with us. Healing means revealing that our human wounds are most intimately connected with the suffering of God himself. To be a living memory of Jesus Christ, therefore, means to reveal the connections between our small sufferings and the great story of God's suffering in Jesus Christ, between our little life and the great life of God with us. By lifting our painful forgotten memories out of the egocentric, individualistic, private sphere, Jesus Christ heals our pains. He connects them with the pain of all humanity, a pain he took upon himself and transformed. To heal, then, does not primarily mean to take pains away but to reveal that our pains are part of a greater pain, that our sorrows are part of a greater sorrow, that our experience is part of the great experience.[20]

Nouwen calls us to a realization that as we endure our own grief and sorrow, we are also participating in the pain of our Savior, Jesus Christ—the one who suffered on behalf of all humanity, a man of sorrows, acquainted with our grief (Isa 53:3a). In the same way, we are also connected to the pain of all humanity. It is a communal pain, a collective pain. A pain caused by our separation by sin from the divine, and a pain caused by the living of every day life in an imperfect, fallen world.

> What pain have you endured?
>   . . . are you currently enduring?
> *Might it be that God wants to use that pain to connect you*
>   *to both his Son and to others?*

I once danced a piece that was born in the midst of a long season of pain. It was a spiritual season of waiting—very much a season of travail. A season where God's voice was "*oh so silent*" and my soul cried out at my own sense of separation from the Lord. I often wept as I created, and what I created was not so much a dance as it was a dramatic representation of my soul wrestling with God. The piece was symbolic of my own pain. I hesitated to present it, but I finally relented.

The day I danced this piece it was standing-room-only at chapel, with many visitors due to a guest speaker that day. I felt very vulnerable as I placed my picture of pain in front of all these people. After I danced, I walked to the back of the room, and the speaker rose and took her place behind the podium. As she shared her testimony of a life filled with suffering, I understood why I had to dance that day. As I danced my pain, it became a symbolic act of the collective, connective pain of all the people in that service.

> Consider your soul's groaning.
>   How is it connected to Christ's?
>   How is it connected to others?

Then read Philippians 3:1—4:1. Ask God to begin to show you how your grief can be a bridge of healing and salvation to others. Don't be afraid of your pain. God can use it. Don't be afraid to be vulnerable with your pain. God will use that too.

Lord, I pray for those who are suffering. I pray that out of their place of pain they will create works of art that will help them connect to the pain of your son Jesus Christ and that speak to the pain of humanity. Moreover, I pray specifically for the people who will then view these works of art. I pray that, as a result of these artists' depictions of their own struggle, others will come to terms with their own wrestling with God. I pray that they will be released from bondage; that they will find freedom; that they will find healing; that they will find love, hope, grace, and mercy. Lord, I know that what often seems to us like a loss can be restored by the mighty hand of God, our Creator. I know that you promise to restore the lost things, for I have read in your word, "*I will restore the years the locusts have eaten*" (Joel 2:25).

I pray that God will restore the loss things in your life; that he will bestow on you a crown of beauty instead of ashes, the oil of gladness instead of mourning, and a garment of praise instead of a spirit of despair. I pray that you will be called an oak of righteousness, a planting of the LORD for the display of his splendor (Isa 61:3).

I pray these things in the Name of Christ, our Redeemer and Restorer,

amen.

Listen to: "The Altar" by Nichole Nordeman

Digging Deeper:
The Turning of the Face

Read: Ezekiel 4:4–17

This story from Ezekiel is part of a series of actions that start at the beginning of chapter 4 and continue through chapter 5. Combined, they tell of the coming siege of Jerusalem and what will happen to the people of God in this siege. As he lies bound on his side, he is enacting the exile and captivity of the people, as well as bearing the punishment of their unfaithfulness to Yahweh.[21] This task of bearing the sins of others was a role that was assigned to the priests, and we see echoes of this in Isaiah 53, the Suffering Servant's Song, where the suffering servant will silently bear the iniquity of all.[22]

Part of our priestly and prophetic roles as artists is to bear the burdens of those to whom we minister. When we are asked to minister through our art at a church, a conference, or other event, do we consider the needs and burdens of those who will witness our artwork? As a minister of the arts, it is imperative that we seek the Lord's direction in prayer before we decide which piece from our repertoire or collection is appropriate and will speak his heart to those in attendance. I have found that when the Lord gives me an idea for a dance, drama, or song, he is always faithful to show me when and where that dance, drama, or song is to be performed.

Moreover, in the case of Ezekiel, he was asked to perform quite a daunting task. I don't know about you, but the thought of lying on my side, bound by ropes, for over fourteen months seems rather overwhelming. How did he eat, drink, and "use the facilities"? If God asked you to do something that seemed impossible to you, would you have the faith and courage of Ezekiel to follow through? God *does* and *will* ask us to bear the burdens of others, and in the case of artistic ministry that burden of bearing is done through our role as priest and prophet communicating through symbolic artistic expression. And sometimes that seems . . . well, unbearable.

But there was one who was willing to bear the most unbearable for the sake of all mankind—the Spotless Lamb. The one without sin was asked to take on all of our sin so that we might be saved. Read Isaiah 53 and consider the task of the Suffering Servant:

He was despised and rejected by men . . .

> ... he took up our infirmities and carried our sorrows ...
> ... he was pierced for our transgressions
> ... crushed by our iniquities.

> *The punishment that brought us peace was upon him*
> *and by his wounds we are healed!*

When our task seems daunting and impossible, "Let us fix our eyes on Jesus, the author and perfecter of our faith, who for the joy set before him endured the cross, scorning its shame, and sat down at the right hand of the throne of God" (Heb 12:2).

What strikes me most about the passage in Ezekiel is God's command to the prophet: "Turn your face toward the siege" (v. 7). As he bore their sins, he also had to face the city of Jerusalem under siege—God's holy city being defaced and defiled by the armies of Babylon. How Ezekiel's heart must have been breaking as he watched and prophesied to his people! I imagine, over the course of fourteen months, there were times when tears streamed down the prophet's face as he watched the destruction of God's city and temple.

It makes me wonder: Did Christ also turned his face towards the city of Jerusalem as he hung on a cross outside the city walls? Did his cross face the city or did he have to strain his neck to turn and see? And down through history, does he still turn his face to see when someone says "Yes" to him? Does he turn to see the joy set before him in the face of a child, a man, a woman who has also turned to see him and to acknowledge him as Lord and Savior seated at the right hand of God?

> *Consider how he turns his face ...*
> *... to you.*

Lord, my God, when I consider the cost of your obedience, I am deeply and profoundly humbled. How can it be that you, my King, would take my place? That you would turn your face—your heart—towards me and die in my stead? I am reminded of the words of Charles Wesley and my heart joins in his song:

> And can it be that I should gain
> An interest in the Savior's blood?
> Died he for me, who caused his pain—
> For me, who him to death pursued?

Amazing love! How can it be,
That Thou, my God, shouldst die for me?[23]

Yes, Jesus, how can it be? As you turn your beautiful face towards me, I bow low before you, for you alone are worthy of my adoration and worship.
In your precious Name, amen.

Listen to: "You Are My King" by Billy James Foote

Endnotes

1. Schroeder, *Embodied Prayer*, 54.
2. Taylor, *Time to Dance*, 11. Emphasized quote is the same.
3. Kane, "Shaping Liturgical Dance," 123.
4. Begbie, *Voicing Creation's Praise*, 249.
5. DeSola, *Spirit Moves*, 147.
6. Rognlien, *Experiential Worship*, 131.
7. Gire, *Windows*, 16–17, as quoted by Rognlien. Rognlien's and Gire's books are great resources for ideas to incorporate creative arts into worship.
8. Miller, "Jeremiah," 683.
9. Lindblom, *Prophecy*, 172.
10. Blenkinsopp, *Ezekiel*, 34.
11. Schroeder, *Embodied Prayer*, 114.
12. George Matheson, "O Love That Will Not Let Me Go," public domain, 1882. Quote from the Church of Scotland magazine *Life and Work*, January 1882.
13. Thompson, *Jeremiah*, 363.
14. Ibid., 365.
15. Thomas Ken, "Praise God from Whom All Blessings Flow," public domain, 1674.
16. Kovacs, *Dancing into the Anointing*, 53.
17. Alves, quoted by Waggoner, *Fairy Tale Faith*, 45.
18. Blenkinsopp, *Ezekiel*, 92.
19. Ibid.
20. Nouwen, *Living Reminder*, 24–25.
21. Blenkinsopp, *Ezekiel*, 35.
22. Ibid.
23. Charles Wesley, "And Can It Be That I Should Gain?," public domain, 1738.

six

Dancing in Your Prayer Closet

*" . . . go into your room, close the door
and pray to your Father . . ."*

M Y PRAYER CLOSET IS big. In fact, it's probably the biggest room in the house. You see, my prayer closet is my basement. That's where I go to dance. I share the space with some old toys, our workout equipment, and my son's new drum set. The walls are concrete block, and a layer of indoor/outdoor carpeting separates me from cold cement floors. It's not beautiful by any means, but it has a CD player and a large mirror left over from a bathroom renovation a few years back. Some of my deepest prayers have been prayed here in this modest space; for it is in this space that I have room to move, to dance out my prayers, to explore, to create.

Connected to Our Source

As Christian artists it is imperative that we spend time with the Master Creator. We cannot create without inspiration, without a source, without a divine spark to ignite us. How can we create something that intentionally displays the glory of God if we have no relationship with God in the first place? Yes, we have all witnessed masterpieces that have been created apart from God that still speak of God in spite of the artist's distance from his or her Source. I'm not saying it *can't* be done. What I'm saying is that as *Christian* artists, it *shouldn't* be done.

We must be connected to the Source of our creativity if we are to create that which is truly life giving and life changing. We must understand his love for us if we are to communicate that love to others. We must know God in all his glory if we are to reveal that glory. We must have a living, breathing relationship with Jesus Christ if we are to be his hands and feet through our artistry or medium. Prayer is one of the most vital ways in which we spend time with God. It isn't an option. It is to be *our way of life*. This is our communication vehicle for conversation with the Divine.

The Prayer Life of the Artist

In the last chapter we focused on the artist's role as prophet, or one who communicates *for* God *to* the people. In this chapter we focus on our prayer life, as those who communicate *to* God *for* the people or ourselves. And this isn't just another book that will tell you to pray. My focus is to help you learn to pray as an artist prays. This is about using the creative process as a prayer language whereby we worship, commune, intercede, contemplate, ask, and plead through our art form.

Stephanie Butler describes the communication of the dance minister as being "bilingual," including both a "*vocal* prayer language" and a "*body* prayer language."[1] Remember our study of symbolic action as including an action (body) accompanied by a word (vocal) for prophetic purposes. Now the two are combined for prayer purposes as we cry out to God. And this is not merely a one-way conversation: the Spirit speaks, too. Scripture tell us that "the Spirit himself intercedes for us with groans that words cannot express" (Rom 8:26). For me, when I dance, it moves beyond my words to my spirit. As I dance, my spirit begins to pray through movements, and the movements become those groans that cannot be expressed. For me, when I run out of words, my movements become my prayer, and I know the Father sees and hears. Worship, and the movements that accompany it, become the groans of my spirit as "deep calls to deep" (Ps 42:7).

But how does this apply to the non-dancing artist? Psychologist and dancer Sara Savage proposes that it is through our bodies and its related movements that we learn about both ourselves and Christ. She states:

> Movement is . . . one of the first languages through which we gain personal knowledge, and as a result, the capacity for propositional knowledge. Hence it is appropriate (perhaps even necessary?) that we use movement to enrich our personal knowledge of Christ

(whom we must approach by faith with our whole selves, not just our intellect). Movement is a language that connects us to our bodies, and to our emotions which resonate within our physical bodies.[2]

Think about your own creative process and ask, "How does it require my body?" The person in drama doesn't have to make a big leap of imagination here. Your work requires lots of movement, in addition to the many other aspects of your art—character development, costumes, voice inflection—that depend on the body. But what about the other arts? A writer studies, imagines, jots down notes, and through movement puts pen to paper (or fingers to keyboard) to create poetry and prose. The photographer stoops and bends to get just the right angle, adjusting the lights, snapping photos by pressing down a tiny button that works the shutter. The artist paints bold strokes across a huge canvas or etches away in tiny lines to get just the right shadows and contrast. The singer relies on vocal cords and breath control. The instrumentalist relies on fingers, breath, and all sorts of body parts! Next time you are in the process of creating, pay attention to your body and how you use it in your creative process. What is it telling you? And are you listening?

Truly it's not just the body, but the entire being that is involved in the creative process. Love the Lord your God with all your heart, soul, mind, and strength, commanded Christ (Mark 12:30). He recognized, both because he himself was human and because he created us, that we are whole persons. We should create with our whole being. In the words of Robert VerEecke, "God chose to be incarnated in creation and, in Jesus, speaks the incarnation language of the body. God knows and hears the cry of the whole person—not merely the spoken word, but also movement, reaching, or touching. It is in the expression of prayer that comes from the whole person that one discovers the presence of a *living, moving, creative* God."[3]

As we engage our entire selves into the creative process, we become *fully engaged*. And in that full engagement, our hearts begin to cry out to God. Carla DeSola says, "You have a desire to pray, yet there are no words. Perhaps the Holy Spirit, groaning within its temple, your body (1 Cor 6) is teaching you a new language. We read in Isaiah that the word of the Lord does not return empty. It runs though the earth and heavens, changing, moving, taking flesh."[4] Prayer is an experience of full engagement. Sue Monk Kidd says, "Prayer isn't strictly a mental activity any more that it's strictly an emotional activity. It's an experience of the *whole* being."[5] Kidd writes of a time in her spiritual journey of dark despair. It was in that time that she began to dance her prayers. She describes her experience:

> Some days, when I was all alone in the house, I danced, letting my body express itself, reverencing its movements, delighting in its energies, and being present to its rhythms. I was freeing it to be. The Bible says, after all, that there's a "time to dance" (Eccl 3:4). My dancing became a kind of contemplative movement, a prayer that began to help me integrate me, to knit my body back to my soul. Slowly I experienced a new "communion" with my lost heart and my lost body.[6]

What if we approached our artwork and creations with this same mindset? Reverencing our movements as we paint, delighting in our energies as we act, and being present to our rhythms as we write or sing?

A New Way to Pray

Perhaps you've never thought of your creative process as prayer. Perhaps you have been just going through the motions, so to speak. But think about it: what if every time you approached your artwork, form, or medium, you began with a prayer and continued to pray throughout the process, not necessarily through words, but through your whole being in a state of ongoing prayer? Body prayer, mindful prayer, heart prayer, soul prayer? Full engagement prayer? What does that look like for you? For your art form?

Matt Durbin majored in art at our local university.[7] He has painted at our church services as well as other services on campus and around the region. As you watch him create, it is as if you are watching someone deeply in prayer. Does he mindfully pray as he creates? I don't know. I *do know* he prayerfully plans before he paints, and I suspect that attitude of prayer instinctively follows him as he puts brush to canvas.

It is my prayer for you that as a sacred artist you begin to realize that your creative act *is* a prayer; that this creative act has the power to evoke the physical and emotional healing necessary to maintain a spirit of wholeness, joy, and strength; that this creative act is part of a faith that moves mountains; and that this "moving faith" presses you forward. In the words of worship leader Darlene Zschech, "You can't break down things in your life by standing still. You must advance—take ground—move."[8] For the Christian artist, this statement is a literal command with physical actions. "For many, the spirit speaks through movement, not words," states Linda Goen, proponent of the creative arts in worship. She continues: "Dance may reach all of us in some way because the connections we make in movement are more pure, without the analytical thought processes that come into play when we speak."[9]

Worship minister Heather Clark applies this thought to *all the arts*: "There is something in the intellect that art bypasses—going straight to spirit, allowing the person to receive even without the mind a certain spiritual understanding."[10] She also applies this to the observer: "The arts are a doorway to a person's soul. They go past the mind and minister to the deep places of a person's spirit."[11] As God is able to bypass our mind and commune directly with our spirit, he can begin to deal with our heart. According to Trevor Hart, "Art draws us deeper and further, takes us beyond the surface in some sense to see or experience something which otherwise remains hidden from us."[12] This is true for the artist, for those who watch as he or she creates, and even for those who view the finished product.

Growing Up into Children

As the heart of God speaks and ministers to the heart of an individual, they find freedom as they are transformed into what God intended. James Fowler speaks of this process as *conversion*, and it is a necessary component for a person to walk in their true calling or *vocation*. This conversion is not a one-time experience, but an *ongoing process*. He says:

> Conversion . . . means accepting, at a depth of heart that is truly liberating, that our worth, our value, our grounding as children of God is *given* as our birthright. It means embracing the conviction that we are known, loved, supported, and invited to partnership in being with one who from all eternity intended us and who desires our love and friendship. . . . It is falling in love with God . . . making an attachment to the passion of Jesus the Christ.[13]

He goes on to say that the Eastern Orthodox religion describes this ongoing process of conversion as "the gracious gift of a divine 'synergy,'" and later, that this "synergy means the release of a quality of creativity and energy that manifests our likeness to the restored image of God in us."[14] Yes! Creativity that helps others and ourselves to be restored to the image of God!

This conversion, divine synergy, or transformation comes to the artist, in part, as he or she prays and groans through movement, through the act of creating, through the imagination of the mind and spirit; as the artist expresses his or her worship, love, and adoration, as well as his or her pain, loneliness, and desolation through art; and as he or she releases that which is bound within them kicking and screaming to be released. With the heart of a true dancer, Clark describes it this way:

> There is something that rises up in the heart of a dancer, something that clapping and singing can't fully express. As the dancer is obedient, and follows the desire to express worship in movement, there is a drawing closer to God that occurs. When a dancer is moved by the Spirit to step out, his or her eyes are totally fixed on Jesus; a beautiful intimacy results from this worshipful obedience. . . . We dance because we are in love with Jesus. We dance because the Bible tells us to. . . . We dance to make war. We dance to celebrate the goodness of God. We dance to lament. We dance because we can't help it. And we dance to express outwardly what is going on inwardly. Dance is a manifestation of what is happening in our hearts towards God.[15]

I believe these sentiments could be stated by every artist in their own medium or language:

We *create* because we are in love with Jesus.

We *play music* because the Bible tells us to.

We *paint* to make war.

We *act* to celebrate the goodness of God.

We *write* to lament.

We *sing* because we can't help it.

We create to express *outwardly* what is going on *inwardly.*

Art is a manifestation of what is happening in our hearts towards God.

Digging Deeper into Praying through the Creative Process

When I was writing much of this chapter, I was working on a dance for a graduation ceremony at the seminary I attended. The song was "Show Me Your Glory" by Cindy Cruse-Ratcliff and Israel Houghton, and the lyrics of the song are a plea to the Lord to reveal his glory to his people.[16] As I created, the song became the prayer of my own heart, and as I danced, my prayer was lifted to the throne room of God. The words became my own as I sought the Lord's face. As I moved, my spirit prayed that I would indeed see his glory, that I would fall to my knees under the weight of it, and that I would look up to see his beautiful face as he reveals himself to me. As

I created I prayed that in that moment I would be united with the One who knew me before he created the heavens and earth and that his perfect love would help me love him more perfectly in return. I prayed that as he continues to transform me into his perfect likeness he can then use me to transform others through the power of his mercy, love, and grace. Let that be your prayer, as well, as you imagine, as you dream, as you prepare, and as you create.

The devotions for this chapter are somewhat different in that they are not studies based on Scripture passages. Instead they rely on different methods of prayer. With each one you will be asked to pray in a different way. You might end up spending several days in one method. Don't feel pressure to make your way through these methods quickly. If you need to spend more time in a method, feel free. Spend as much time as you need and then move on to the next. My own prayer is that God will meet you in a very powerful way as you meditate on him and as you use your creative process as a way to meet the Creator of all creativity.

Digging Deeper: Dancing in Your Prayer Closet
Lectio Divina
Praying through the Psalms
All Prayers in One
Heart's Cry through Song
Interceding through the Creative Process

Digging Deeper:
Lectio Divina

I grew up in church. I've heard Bible stories all my life. Every Sunday the teacher would place Jesus, Moses, or Mary up on a blue flannel board. As she told a story, other people and animals would appear until the board was filled with flannel-backed cardboard characters. As a child those characters were a part of my reality, but it wasn't until much later that I began to connect with them, to understand them as real people who struggled with God, faith, and a world turned upside down. As I matured in my own faith, I learned new ways of approaching my Bible and the stories it contains. A book that profoundly changed the way I read my Bible is *Shaped by the Word: The Power of Scripture in Spiritual Formation*, by M. Robert Mulholland Jr. As I slowed down and placed myself in the passages before me, I began to see the Scriptures anew. My flannel-board Jesus came to life as an actual living, breathing man who walked this earth.

Lectio divina encourages us to do the same. *Lectio divina* is not technically a method of prayer, but a method of reading Scripture. It does, however, lend itself to reading the Scriptures in a very prayer-like fashion. So we will start here with the Scriptures, for it is God's voice to his people, the way he has communicated to us for thousands of years.

Lectio divina (pronounced lex-ee-o dih-vee-nah) is Latin. *Lectio* means "reading" and *divina* means "sacred" or "holy." So essentially it is "sacred reading" or "holy reading." While the method of using Scripture meditatively was most likely used by the desert fathers of the early first century, *lectio divina* is attributed to St. Benedict (c. 480–c. 550 CE), father of the Benedictine monasteries. *The Rule of St. Benedict* revolved around three essentials: prayer, work, and *lectio divina*, so it was a vital aspect to each day. The four steps that are used in *lectio divina* were spelled out by Guigo II (c. 1115–c. 1198 CE) in his book *Scala Claustralium* (*The Ladder of Monastics*).[17] They are: *lectio*—reading; *meditatio*—mediation; *oratio*—prayer; and *contemplatio*—contemplation.

Psalm 119:9–16 poses a question and gives us this wisdom:

> How can a young man keep his way pure?
> By living according to your word.
> I seek you with all my heart;
> Do not let me stray from your commands.
> I have hidden your word in my heart that I might not sin against you.

Praise be to you, O LORD;
Teach me your decrees.
With my lips I recount all the laws that come from your mouth.
I rejoice in following your statutes as one rejoices in great riches.

I meditate on your precepts and consider your ways.
I delight in your decrees;
I will not neglect your word.

As Christian artists, we must stay grounded in his word. But simply reading is not nearly enough. We must become a part of the biblical narrative—part of The Story. The very last verses of the Bible read:

He who is the faithful witness to all these things says,
"Yes, I am coming soon!"
Amen! Come, Lord Jesus!
May the grace of the Lord Jesus be with God's holy people.
(Rev 22:20–21, NLT)

This affirms that The Story is true, that The Story continues, and that we are a part of the continuing Story as God's holy people. As we read our Bibles meditatively, it allows us to realize our part in The Story—how our lives are like Abraham, Ruth, Gideon, and Rahab—and how we too can have faith in the midst of the stories of our lives, woven and connected to this beautiful ongoing story of the saints of God. This method of *lectio divina* helps us slow down and enter into this great story, to apply it to our lives, and hopefully, as artists, continue to retell it in our own words, mediums, and art forms.

Find a quiet place, a sacred space. Grab the most "readable" Bible you own. Ask God into the moment. Search out a passage to which you believe he is leading you. Follow these steps as you read:[18]

1. *Lectio*—reading. Read the passage slowly. Read it again, perhaps out loud this time. Pay attention to what grabs your attention. Is there a word or phrase that rises above the rest? Read it again, paying attention to that word or phrase within the entire passage.

2. *Meditatio*—mediation. Dig deeper into the text. What is God really saying? What is Jesus doing? How is the Holy Spirit involved in this passage? What underlies the story? Why is this passage important? What aspects of the culture or people are important? Don't get bogged down with outside resources or commentaries

here—just what you know off the top of your head. You might even want to place yourself in the story as one of the characters or a bystander. As you ponder these things, pay attention to the feelings it evokes in your spirit.

3. *Oratio*—prayer. Begin a conversation with God as you continue to ponder the passage. Ask him to reveal himself to you through the passage. What is he saying to you *personally* through this passage? Ask him about the emotions that are welling up in you. Where do they come from? What in your spirit is connecting to his spirit in these emotions? What does he want you to understand about him? About yourself? About your relationship to each other?

4. *Contemplatio*—contemplation. Contemplation is from *contemplari*, "to gaze attentively, observe." When I think of contemplation I think of Mary, the mother of Jesus, who treasured up the things that surrounded the birth of Christ and pondered them in her heart (Luke 2:19). She wasn't quick to make a decision; she waited. She thought on the events and the things that were said. She considered them with full and deep thought and reflection. She allowed it to be what it was—nothing more, nothing less. If in step three you realize that God is simply telling you he loves you, then contemplate that love, reflect on that love, rest in that love.

Allow God to move into your space, your mind, and your heart as you read his word in this manner. For some of us, this process is second nature. For others it is new and will require some time to adjust, to learn, to wait on God's word to reveal itself. Some folks will get lost in the passage and find an hour has past. Others will struggle to go beyond ten minutes. Just let it be what it is. Be patient with yourself if this doesn't come naturally. Don't worry or struggle. Just be. God will guide and direct you. He will teach you and instruct you, in and through his word.

And may you be caught up in God's unending love story as you read.

Listen to: "Word of God Speak" by Mercy Me

Digging Deeper:
Praying through the Psalms

The book of Psalms is filled with prayers. Prayers of praise, anguish, joy, sorrow, contentment, anger. The prayers found in the Psalms have carried me through many seasons in my journey. When I couldn't find my own words, they became my prayers, and I read them repeatedly. I posted them on my bathroom mirror. I sang them. I memorized them. And when that season came to an end, I found another and repeated the process.

In times of great longing, I prayed:

> One thing I ask of the LORD,
> this is what I seek:
> that I may dwell in the house of the LORD
> all the days of my life,
> to gaze upon the beauty of the LORD
> and to seek him in his temple. (Ps 27:4)

When I was afraid, I prayed:

> He reached down from on high and took hold of me;
> he drew me out of deep waters.
> He brought me out into a spacious place;
> he rescued me because he delighted in me. (Ps 18:16, 19)

When I needed a battle cry, I prayed:

> Who is this King of glory?
> The LORD strong and mighty,
> the LORD mighty in battle.
> Lift up your heads, O you gates;
> lift them up, you ancient doors,
> that the King of glory may come in.
> Who is he, this King of glory?
> The LORD Almighty—
> he is the King of glory. (Ps 24:8–10)

When I was in the desert, I prayed:

> O God, you are my God, earnestly I seek you;
> my soul thirsts for you, my body longs for you,
> in a dry and weary land where there is no water. (Ps 63:1)

When trouble came my way, I prayed:

> He who dwells in the shelter of the Most High
> will rest in the shadow of the Almighty.
> I will say of the LORD,
> "He is my refuge and my fortress, my God, in whom I trust."
> Surely he will save you from the fowler's snare
> and from the deadly pestilence.
> He will cover you with his feathers,
> and under his wings you will find refuge;
> his faithfulness will be your shield and rampart. (Ps 91:1–4)

I was praying the Psalms.

Often when we read the Bible, passages rise to the surface and strike a chord in our heart. They speak the very thing we're thinking but have been afraid or unable to voice. When I have no words, I go to the book of Psalms. I read until my heart finds a voice. Sometimes passages I've read a thousand times come alive for the first time, and I discover a new meaning that I had never seen. In that moment, they speak the unarticulated words of my spirit. In one of my Bibles, there are wide, lined margins in the book of Psalms. These lined margins are nowhere else in my Bible. They encourage me to journal, to compose my own psalm, to express what I'm hearing from God. They encourage me to stop and pray.

When we pray through the Psalms, we allow them to be our voice. So this method is particularly helpful when we don't have the words to pray ourselves. As artists, we can take this a step further and use creativity to help us pray our psalms. Throughout the seasons of my life, when a specific psalm rose to the surface, that psalm became my inspiration. I would create music and sing it. I might write a drama centered on that passage. I might create a dance to it. It doesn't matter what medium you work with. Whatever that medium is becomes the way you put shape and form to the words before you. Praying through the Psalms isn't some complicated reading schedule. It is simply reading the Psalms throughout the many seasons of your life and letting the words of these beautiful songs rise to the surface and invade your creative thought processes.

Let the words of this beautiful psalm be our prayer:

> Your word, O Lord, is eternal, everlasting, and ceaseless.
> It stands firm in the heavens, on the earth, in all of creation.
> Your faithfulness continues through all generations,

from Adam and Eve to this very present day.
You established the earth, and it endures.
Your word is a lamp unto our feet and a light for our paths;
Let it guide us without falter or fail.
Your statutes are our heritage forever, until the end of our days.
They are the joy of our hearts, the song of our spirits.
You are our refuge and our shield.
We put our hopes, our dreams, our desires in your word,
and in you alone, O God our Redeemer and Friend. Amen.
(from Ps 119, paraphrase)

Now, pick up a Bible. Ask God to help you as you seek. Sift through the Psalms until you find a psalm—*the* psalm—that speaks your heart. Write it out. Post it somewhere you can see every day—your bathroom mirror, your desk, your kitchen sink, your easel, your studio. Read and reread it. Let it sink into the depths of your being. Let it be your voice. Then, begin to create to it. Let it illustrate your heart. Paint to it. Rewrite it with your own words. Develop it into a story. Photograph it. Memorize it and speak it as a monologue. Sing it. Dance it. Portray it. Create it.

Pray it.

Listen to: "Lead Me to the Rock" by Stephen Hurd

Digging Deeper:
All Prayers in One

Throughout my prayer life, certain prayers have risen above the rest and have stayed with me. I repeat them—again and again. Not as mantras or route prayers, but as real prayers. Prayers that remind me of where I've been and where he's taking me. Prayers that remind me of who he is and who I am. Prayers that bring me home when I've strayed. Prayers that keep me grounded and anchored.

At one point in my Christian walk I was praying for discernment. Not that I hadn't prayed for it before, but I was at a point in my ministry where I needed an extra measure because every decision I made as a ministry leader was being questioned: "Did you pray about that?" and "Did God reveal this to you or are you speaking from your own wisdom?" and "What did God say about this?" As a result of this constant questioning, it became increasingly difficult to make any decision for fear of making the wrong one, of not listening or hearing the voice of God correctly. I remember mulling *everything* over in prayer—I mean *everything*! I couldn't even make the simplest of decisions without calling myself or my decisions into question.

About the time I was nearly paralyzed by the prayerfulness of each decision, God lead me to an audio series by Graham Cooke on discerning the will of God.[19] In that teaching he talked about how God has given us a mind, intelligence, and the ability to make sound decisions. Through this teaching, God affirmed in me the fact that he had given me wisdom and a strong foundation of Scripture. God declared that he had already given me discernment and that I was using that discernment in every decision I made—even those decisions I didn't take directly to him in prayer. While that season was truly testing, it allowed several prayers to rise to the surface and become a part of who I was and how I made decisions in life and ministry. Throughout that season my prayers went something like this:

Lord, I want to be able to see things as you see them. I want to look at a situation and see what you see. In the natural, I want to see the spiritual. I want to have "spiritual eyesight." I want to see people through your eyes. I want to love them like you love them. I want to have your heart towards them. I want to be your hands as I reach out to them and your feet as I bring them the gospel of peace. I want a new level of discernment so that I can see beyond what is apparent to what is hidden. I want to see your kingdom come here on earth, and I want things on earth to be as they are in heaven. I want your will—in my life, in my ministry, in the lives of my husband and children, in the lives of the people of my church. I want your will to be done above my will. I want to see earth through heaven's eyes.

After awhile, these prayers simply became:

Your eyes.

Your heart.

Your kingdom.

Your will.

Notice the number of times I say "I want" in my first prayer. Seems like a pretty self-centered prayer—yet it is not. Yes, it is all about me—*me* bowing down, *me* surrendering, *me* giving up, *me* giving in. Yet it is all about God—*him* being elevated, *him* taking over, *him* revealing, *him* being him. And when I distill it down, when I sift it out, it is all him, not me: *his* eyes, *his* heart, *his* kingdom, *his* will. I must decrease so that God might increase.

My professor and friend Terry Wardle first introduced me to the idea of "all prayers in one" as a prayer method during this season of my journey. You might have heard of "centering prayer" or "breath prayer," and this prayer method is very similar to these. In this method you allow your prayers to be sifted until the fullness of the prayer comes to the surface. The root, the essence, rises above all the other words and your prayer is stated in a few, simple words. As Wardle taught our class about this prayer method—about praying all prayers in one—I realized I was doing just that. That the "I want" was being distilled and sifted out of my prayers, until all that was left was him. That the essence and root of my prayer was rising above all the other words.

What are your prayers—the ones you repeat over and over? Go back through your journals. What themes do you see throughout? When it's all said and done, what's most important? Begin to sift through these prayers. What is their essence? What is the root of these prayers? What words rise to the surface?

The most amazing thing about these prayers is that when we pray them, God knows all the others prayers that are bound up in this one prayer! He knows all the words that have been spilled at his feet. He sees all the tears and has recorded each one (Ps 56:8). He knows every word spoken and unspoken. He knows the fullness of each word. He knows the lifetime of prayers that lie behind it. He knows the lifetime of prayers yet to be prayed ahead of it. The prayer speaks of who he is, what he's done, and what he's going to do. The prayer speaks of your essence and of his essence.

As you weave all prayers into one, can you now create something that depicts it?

What does your prayer look like?
What does it sound like in poetry or prose?
Can it be photographed or filmed?
Can it be set to music?
As you sit down at your easel,
as you enter your studio,
as you sit before your wheel or loom,
can you pray this prayer?
How does it move your pen or your paintbrush?
How does it spill into your work?
Can you sing it?
Can you play it?
Can you allow it to lead you as you create?

I pray that as your prayers are distilled into one that God will meet you there; that you will have full assurance that he hears you; that he knows every prayer of your heart.

And, that he will answer you.

Listen to: "Hear Our Prayers" by The Glorious Unseen

Digging Deeper:
Heart's Cry through Song

I love music. I love the old hymns. I love the contemporary Christian songs of this generation. I love the searing guitars in hard rock. I love the magnificent strings in classical music. I love the banjoes and harmonicas of folk rock. There is something about music that pulls at your heart, that sheds light on the state of your being, that opens it up for God to enter in. I love music. It soothes the soul. Yet it is also somewhat dangerous because it makes us vulnerable.

Have you ever noticed the lyrics to some of the songs you sing at church, especially the ones about surrender? They are deep, heart-felt prayers. And we often sing them lightly, with no regard to what we're really saying. Yet as we sing them, we give God permission to enter in and change those things we'd rather leave unchanged or expose those things we'd rather keep hidden. The words we sing leave us open and vulnerable. Yet they leave us open and vulnerable before a gentle, loving Abba God, a God who longs to mold us into the beautiful image of his Son, Jesus Christ.

If we really consider the fact that our songs are prayers, then we must also consider what we are praying through these songs. Henri Nouwen once wrote:

> Praying is no easy matter. It demands a relationship in which you allow someone other than yourself to enter into the very center of your person, to see there what you would rather leave in darkness, and to touch there what you would rather leave untouched. Why would you really want to do that? Perhaps you would let the other cross your inner threshold to see something or touch something, but to allow the other into that place where your intimate life is shaped—that is dangerous and calls for defense.[20]

I love Nouwen's transparency in this. You may not feel this way when you pray "light" prayers, but when you pray the "heavy" ones, you understand what he's getting at here. When we pray soul-bearing, heart-cleansing, depth-unburying prayers, we are giving God permission to enter the darkest, most hidden places of our hearts. That can be unnerving, frightening even.

Whether or not we recognize it, our songs are prayers. And some of those prayers are very deep and transparent. And they invite God to do some very life-changing things. Think for a moment of your favorite song of surrender. Consider the prayer of the song. Odds are, it's a very intense prayer. What it is inviting God to do?

If we really understood the depth of the prayers we sing, would we still sing them? Do we really want to surrender all to God and let him in to the very depths of our hearts in this way? Next time you are in worship, really look at the words you are singing. Don't just sing along; pray along. And as artists and creative Christians, we can lead the way in understanding the depth of the prayers we sing.

I often ask the people in my embodied prayer group to find their "heart's song"—a song that speaks their heart in the place where they are in their journey.

What song do you play over and over?
What song speaks your prayer?
When you have no words,
when you've prayed all you can pray,
what song speaks for you?

We all have these songs—perhaps you even have two or three. Perhaps there's one that speaks for your whole lifetime of prayers. Perhaps there's one that speaks how you feel today, in this very moment.

Think over those songs. Which one speaks your heart in this moment? Today, I want you to take that song and create to it. Put it on in your studio, at your desk, and allow it to move you. Allow it to be your prayer time today. No words of your own are necessary. Allow the song to speak for you. Allow the song to open your heart so that you can pour out and God can pour in. Where does it lead your body? Where does it lead your paintbrush or pen? What does it lead you to photograph or film?

This devotion is brief—intentionally brief. You know the song: the one that's been tugging at your heartstrings. Listen to it. Let God take your hand and lead you in a dance, a dance of creativity and discovery. Let him bear. Let him cleanse. Let him unbury. Let him mold. Let him love you as only your Abba God can. Listen!

It is good to praise the LORD
and make music to your name, O Most High,
proclaiming your love in the morning
and your faithfulness at night. (Ps 92:1-2)

Can you hear it? It's the song of your loving Creator.
Follow your heart.
It will lead you.
He will lead you.

Listen to your own heart's song

Digging Deeper:
Interceding through the Creative Process

sk yourself,

"Who am I in ministry for?"
"Why did God call me into this?"

Have you ever thought about these questions? Ultimately we are called into ministry for God—to make his glory and his kingdom real and tangible on this earth. But why? God's glory isn't a selfish glory. If God wanted glory all for himself, he'd stick with the angels. That's their job. Why is it important that *we* give him glory? Because we make him real. We give him hands and feet. We keep him alive. We help others see the invisible, touch the intangible, sense the mysterious.

In our roles as priests of God's kingdom, we must be other-focused. So many times as artists, we get wrapped up in the inward, self-focused examination that helps us create from the depths of who we are. But we cannot stay there. At some point we need to realize that our creative works give life, breath, and freedom to others through the power of the Holy Spirit's life-giving power. This priestly role calls us to a life of intercession.

The brokenness of the world around us calls us to be intercessors. If Christ's kingdom is to come and be established here on earth, our prayers must be lifted to the throne. They must rise like incense. In Revelation 5 we find the creatures and elders encircling the throne of God with golden bowls of incense. Scripture tells us these bowls are filled with the prayers of the saints—that's us! That's *our prayers!* All of them collected and presented to the Glorious One on the throne as a sacrifice of worship. Our collective prayers rise like incense to meet the nostrils of God!

There was a time during our church's short history that I was called to deep intercession on behalf of our flailing congregation. Many times I had no words left to pray, but my spirit continued on without words. I would often weep before the throne of God for reasons unknown to me. There were no words, yet my spirit would groan and cry out to God on behalf of our church. Sometimes I would retreat to my basement—my "prayer closet"—and dance songs of warfare and intercession for the people and leadership of my church. I don't believe I had ever prayed so hard in all my life. It often took a physical toll on my body. Pat Chen talks about the groaning of the spirit in intercession:

This groaning is similar to childbirth: 'For we know that the whole creation groans and suffers the pains of childbirth together until now.' All of creation, the whole creation groans and suffers the pains of childbirth. We ourselves groan within ourselves, waiting eagerly for our adoption as sons, the redemption of our body. Our groaning is touching the creative purposes that God has in the earth. Our groaning is touching the glorious part of completion and redemption of all things at Christ's coming. We groan because our spirits know very well that a day is coming when they will find completion and perfect union in God. We groan as we await that day, and our groans actually reach into the purposes of God and speed up the process.[21]

And the Scriptures also remind us that we are not alone in our intercession. Christ stands as our intercessor, our mediator! First Timothy 2:5 states that Christ stands alone as the only mediator between God and man; Isaiah 53:12 says that Christ intercedes for the transgressors; Hebrews 7:25 says that Christ lives to intercede for those who come to God; and Romans 8:34 shows Jesus at the right hand of God interceding for us. As we lift our hands in intercession like Moses (Exod 17:8–16), Christ comes as Aaron and Hur, holding up our hands when we have no strength left to keep praying.

Our role as artists can call us to a unique method of intercession. I truly and deeply believe that our manner of creating, in a prayerful mindset, can be intercession. Once my friend Matt Durbin (who I mentioned earlier in this chapter) was painting at a conference. There was a woman in the audience who had been given up for adoption after her birth mother had already named her, but then realized she couldn't raise her on her own. In recent years she had buried both of her adoptive parents and been estranged from her adopted sister. In the midst of all this loss, her husband left her for another woman. That night she was distraught and crying out for God to give her an answer, to speak to her. She had gone forward for prayer and several people prayed over her, and yet she felt no peace, no answers. She finally returned to her seat in front of Matt's painting. As she raised her tear-filled eyes from her lap and looked to the painting before her, there, she finally saw her answer. Written across Matt's painting were the words from the Gospel of John: "I will not leave you as orphans" (John 14:18a). In that painting, she found all the answers she needed. She heard the voice of God.

What if the next time you created something you paused and prayed not only for God to lead you, but prayed specifically for the person who will be touched by the work you are creating?

Next time you put paintbrush to canvas, pause and pray,

> "Lord, someone who is broken will one day see this painting.
> So, I give this painting over to you.
> I ask you clasp your hand over mine and move this paintbrush
> as you see fit."

Next time you write a song or a script, pause and pray,

> "Abba Father, someone out there needs to hear your voice.
> Please speak through these words."

As you begin to shoot and edit, pause and pray,

> "Jesus Christ, let your image be clear in this work.
> Let the broken and lonely see you reaching out to them."

What if every piece of artwork, song, choreography, script, and film were approached in this manner? What if every time we entered the creative process, we paused and asked God to guide us so that what we were about to create would speak healing and freedom for the people who would one day be touched by it? What if we painted, danced, wrote, sang, played, or acted as if we were praying, interceding, and mediating for a best friend or spouse dying of cancer?

> What if?
> Would it make a difference?
> I believe it would: it does!
> Do you?

Listen to: "Prayers of the Saints" by Dave Barnes

Endnotes

1. Butler, *My Body,* 113.
2. Savage, "Through Dance," 66.
3. VerEecke, "A Vision," 158.
4. DeSola, *Spirit Moves,* 8.
5. Kidd, *When the Heart,* 133.
6. Ibid., 166.
7. Matt Durbin's art can be seen at http://www.mattdurbinart.com.
8. Zschech, *Extravagant Worship,* 51.
9. Goens, *Praising God,* 69.
10. Clark, *Dancing Hand,* 60–61.
11. Ibid., 84.
12. Hart, "Through the Arts," 9.
13. Fowler, *Becoming Adult,* 115.
14. Ibid., 115–16.
15. Clark, *Dancing Hand,* 15–16.
16. Cruse-Ratcliff and Houghton, "Show Me Your Glory," Integrity's Praise, 2001.
17. Jones, *Sacred Way,* 49.
18. Much of this is based on the work of Tony Jones in his book *The Sacred Way.* You can go to his book for further thoughts and reflection on this method. It is also outlined in many other books on spiritual formation and Scripture reading.
19. Graham Cooke's teaching materials are available through Brilliant Book House.
20. Nouwen, *Dance of Life,* 151–52.
21. Chen, *Depths of God,* 62.

seven

Seasons in the Life of the Artist

"For everything there is a season . . ."

IN 1959 AMERICAN FOLK singer Pete Seeger wrote a song based almost entirely on the passage in the third chapter of Ecclesiastes originally written by King Solomon. That song was later made famous by a cover version The Byrds released in 1965, and it reached the top spot on the music charts in the United States. That song of course is "Turn! Turn! Turn! (to Everything There Is a Season)," and I imagine right now you're probably singing those lines in your head. With its ancient text, it holds the record for the #1 hit song with the oldest lyrics. It reminds us that there is a season for everything under heaven.

For Everything a Season

Ecclesiastes is one of several books in what Bible scholars call "wisdom literature"—meant to give wisdom for life and living. It is attributed to King Solomon, the king who cried out to God for wisdom and was granted his prayerful request (1 Kgs 3–4). Here in Ecclesiastes 3:1–8, the famous wise king becomes an artist, in this case a poet, who observes life and its rhythms and sets down this verse so that others may learn from its wisdom.

The wisdom of this passage tells us that there is an ordered pattern to all of creation. Its pairs, in literary terms called *merisms*, are meant to express a sense of the totality of human activity and effort. One activity is not necessarily better than another—they just are the reality of the world in which we find ourselves. According to Old Testament scholar William

Brown, "Each activity . . . has its season, and the seasons themselves have their place in the rhythms of the ever-circling years."[1] *Zeman* is the Hebrew word used here for "season," and it indicates an appointed or predetermined time. It is not haphazard or chaotic. There is a rhythm—an ebb and flow, a wax and wane—and it's all part of the passing seasons of life.

Verse 11 sums up the heart of the book of Ecclesiastes: "He has made everything beautiful in its time. He has also set eternity in the human heart; yet no one can fathom what God has done from beginning to end." Behind all the busyness of human activity, there is still a sense of the eternal. We say to ourselves, "There has got to be more than this!" as we search for meaning and significance in our lives. We cannot grasp the entirety of human affairs and history. We cannot control it either. Yet we try to make sense of it all by seeking traces of eternity, the Divine—that which will last forever in that which will last for only a moment. And the Divine reminds us that *all* is made beautiful in its time, that *all things* work together for his good purposes (Rom 8:28), and that he makes *all things* new (Rev 21:5).

In verses 14 and 15, King Solomon's wisdom continues to lead us in our response. *The Message* translation states it this way (emphasis added):

> I've also concluded that whatever God does,
> that's the way it's going to be, always.
> No addition, no subtraction.
> God's done it and that's it.
> That's so we'll quit asking questions
> and *simply worship in holy fear.*
> Whatever was, is.
> Whatever will be, is.
> That's how it always is with God.

Only God knows the beginning from the end. He alone is sovereign. We're not talking about a fatalist attitude here, but a humble acceptance of his plans and trust in his unfailing love, faithfulness, and sovereignty. We must understand and anticipate the cycles, rhythms, and seasons of life. And as his children we need to realize, understand, and accept those cycles, rhythms, and seasons for ourselves and, more importantly, to help others do the same.

The Seasons of Life

Author Parker Palmer writes of the seasons of life—using the seasons of the natural world (summer, autumn, winter, spring) as a metaphor to help us understand the spiritual and emotional seasons of our lives (abundance, change, loss/death, new beginnings). His thoughts echo that of King Solomon as he examines the "eternal cycle of the seasons." The framework for this chapter is based on his work.[2] I have built on this framework over the years, as I have used this metaphor often in mentoring, spiritual direction, embodied prayer, and small groups. Each season has its avenues for learning, for creativity, and for growth. Each season also comes with its pitfalls and problems. Let's explore each one.

Summer

Summer is the season of joyful abundance. According to Palmer, summer is when there is a "steady state of plenty."[3] This is a season of blessing. Summer is a time for recreation for God delights in our play. It is a time to celebrate for Jesus came that our joy may be complete (John 15:11). Smile more. Laugh more. Observe God's sense of humor. It is a time to restore, refresh, and create anew. As artists this may be a time of great creativity. Keep your eyes open for what he is teaching you.

It is also a time for gratitude. Be careful not to forget about God and his blessings. In Deuteronomy 6:12 we read this warning: "Be careful that you do not forget the Lord, who brought you out of Egypt, out of the land of slavery." It is a *call for remembrance*. God is teaching his people an important lesson: when things are going great, don't forget who it was that brought you here in the first place! For you see the pitfall of summer is that sometimes we miss it when it's happening. We don't count our blessings—we simply take them for granted. And we are called not only to *count* our blessings but also to *share* our blessings. According to Palmer, "abundance is a communal act."[4] This is not a time for hoarding. Our blessings are not mean for us alone—they are meant to be shared with and within our greater community.

More on summer again in a bit, but now we look to autumn.

Autumn

Autumn is a season of change. Summer's abundance begins its slow decay. Early on there is a glorious display of color and beauty, but autumn's early splendor gives way to brown leaves and eventually, barren trees. We watch the leaves change and begin to fall. And the trees, in the words of Palmer, scatter their seeds "with amazing abandon."[5] They show us what it means to let go, to allow what is dead to fall to the ground to make way for future harvest. We see the caterpillar spinning its cocoon and the squirrels gathering their nuts, and we know the death of winter is coming.

Autumn brings with it transition. Of course we know the old adage is that no one likes change. However, we must *anticipate* change—go with the changes taking place around us—*embrace* change. During this transition there is a "letting go" of the way things used to be and adjusting to the new. We need to ask ourselves what God is calling us to let go of. Once we identify those things, we need to grieve our losses, for the heart cannot let go of that which it has not grieved. This too can also be a time of great creativity as you use your creative process as a way to grieve. Putting pen to paper, brush to canvas, movement to song are all useful ways to allow the spirit to mourn.

I also believe that autumn is a time when God plants new seeds deep within—dreams, visions, ideas. They often start small, but pay attention to those small "inklings." They may be pointing towards your future.

And at last the changes of autumn give way to the quiet death of winter.

Winter

Winter is the season of loss and death. Simply put: winter is the time of dying to our old self so the new self can emerge (Col 3:1–10). And while simply put, it is not simply done. For those of us who have experienced our fair share of winters, we know this can be a difficult and painful process. With temporal, earthly eyesight we only see death in its finality, as an end state. However, with eternal, heavenly eyesight, we see death for what it is—a transitional state that leads to resurrection. Christ died, but the tomb could only hold him temporarily. For behind the gravestone, the Miracle of All Miracles was taking place, and resurrection was on the horizon!

The danger of winter is that in our grief over the loss and death of what we hold dear, we forget the promises of rebirth. Remember the disciples.

As they mourned over the loss of their Messiah, they forgot his words of truth and promise. They were shocked when they heard of his resurrection and even mocked the eyewitnesses of his rebirth (Mary Magdalene and the other women at the tomb). But later their eyes were opened and they witnessed Christ for themselves in their very midst.

If we are not careful winter's sorrow can turn to depression—and this is especially true for the sensitive heart of the artist. We must hold on—no, *cleave*—to the truth that God is close to those who mourn:

- Blessed are those who mourn, for they will be comforted. (Matt 5:4)

- The LORD is close to the brokenhearted and saves those who are crushed in spirit. (Ps 34:18)

- He heals the brokenhearted and binds up their wounds. (Ps 147:3)

- The lowly he sets on high, and those who mourn are lifted to safety. (Job 5:11)

God also promises to turn our deepest pain and sorrow into joy:

> Sing the praises of the LORD, you his faithful people;
> praise his holy name.
> For his anger lasts only a moment, but his favor lasts a lifetime;
> *weeping may stay for the night, but rejoicing comes in the morning.*
> When I felt secure, I said, "I will never be shaken."
> LORD, when you favored me,
> you made my royal mountain stand firm;
> but when you hid your face, I was dismayed.
> To you, LORD, I called; to the Lord I cried for mercy:
> "What is gained if I am silenced, if I go down to the pit?
> Will the dust praise you? Will it proclaim your faithfulness?
> Hear, LORD, and be merciful to me; LORD, be my help."
> *You turned my wailing into dancing;*
> *you removed my sackcloth and clothed me with joy,*
> that my heart may sing your praises and not be silent.
> LORD my God, I will praise you forever.
> (Ps 30:4–12, emphasis added)

> They will be like a well-watered garden, and they will sorrow no more. . . . I will turn their mourning into gladness; I will give them comfort and joy instead of sorrow. (Jer 31:12b–13)

Remember the butterfly? Inside its chrysalis, there is a metamorphosis, a transformation, taking place. Even though it appears to be a place of death, of nothingness, of darkness, we know that inside the chrysalis, an incredible change is taking place.

Author Sue Monk Kidd writes beautifully of the winter landscape in her book *When the Heart Waits*.[6] In her own personal journey through the winter of her soul, she happens upon a chrysalis, and it becomes the symbol of her struggle over the next several months as she waits through the stillness of this season. She writes of "the spiritual art of cocooning" and using stillness as a place of creativity. She writes: "Hanging upside down in the heart of the question, we touch the sacred spaces of real becoming."[7]

I love that expression—*the sacred places of real becoming*. I want to "really become" who God intended me to be—as a person and as an artist. It is a sacred place. God has entrusted me with gifts he specifically needs me to bring to this world, and I must hang upside down in all my questions to discover those treasures. The same is true of each of you. As artists we need to explore the chrysalis, the winter of our souls. Let it find expression in our artwork, music, or craft. Creativity that emerges from the dark, quiet places of winter is often the most profound. It carries a depth that others who have endured long, cold winters can see, hear, and recognize.

And while we wait for the deep thaw of winter, we hold to the hope that the miraculous truth of winter is that spring will follow—that the butterfly does *indeed* emerge from her chrysalis beautifully transformed.

Spring

Spring is a season of new beginnings. It is the season of resurrection and rebirth. It is when the new self emerges from the darkness of winter's frozen hold on the landscape of our hearts. "Behold, I make all things new!" says the resurrected Lamb and King, Jesus Christ (Rev 21:5). In spring, all is made new. The spring rains help thaw the frozen ground. Winds blow removing dead limbs from slowly budding trees. Bulbs that have lain dormant begin to surface in a beautiful array of color and vibrancy. Signs of life are all around us.

Yet the danger of spring is that it is often hard to trust that spring has come after the harshness of winter. We never quite know when spring is coming or when it has truly arrived. I live in the Midwest. Between winter and spring, we have several more seasons that aren't on the calendar. They are: more winter, feels like spring but its still winter, almost spring, just one more snowstorm, and not yet spring. Perhaps I'm being facetious, but if you've lived through a spring in the Midwest, you know exactly what I mean. We've even had a snowstorm on April Fools' Day!

You see, the hardest part of the spiritual season of spring is to keep Satan from bringing us down. There is definitely a "thrusting through" that is required of our spirit—like the daffodil pushing up through once frozen ground. This is when perseverance is our trusted ally. Use your art and your creativity to help you thrust through, to emerge from the once seemingly barren landscape of winter.

Did you know that when the butterfly emerges from its chrysalis, it hangs upside down and waits while its wings unfurl, waiting to be filled with moisture stored in its body? The same is true for us. We must wait for all the fullness of winter to soak into our spirit so we can soar into spring.

> *I am impatient.*
> *I take flight too soon and find I cannot fly.*
> *I must wait.*
> *I am too impatient.*
> *Sometimes it still feels like winter.*
> *I must wait—still.*
> But rest assured, *it is spring* and summer is on its way.
> Do you remember summer?
> Now that the seasons have past, do you still remember?

Palmer poetically calls us to remembrance:

Summer is the season when all the promissory notes of autumn and winter and spring come due, and each year the debts are repaid with compound interest. In summer, it is hard to remember that we had ever doubted the natural process, had ever ceded death the last word, had ever lost faith in the powers of new life. Summer is a reminder that our faith is not nearly as strong as the things we profess to have faith in—a reminder that for this single season, at least, we might cease our anxious machinations and give ourselves to the abiding and abundant grace of our common life.[8]

Is It a Season or Just the Weather?

Each season has its purpose and meaning. We must learn the lessons of each season. If we spend our spiritual life longing for summer, then God cannot teach us the lesson of the season in which we currently find ourselves. Kidd urges us to embrace each season and allow our creativity to grow, blossom, and mature. She tells us, "Crises, change, all the myriad upheavals that blister the spirit and leave us groping—they aren't voices simply of pain but also of creativity. And if we would only listen, we might hear such times beckoning us to a season of waiting, to the fertile emptiness.[9] We must embrace our current season, not rush it.

Someone once asked me if the seasons always went in order. As I have studied this metaphor for life, I would have to say yes. However, sometimes the seasons pass so quickly we miss them. Other times a particular season can last for years, and we experience micro-seasons within a season. My most recent spiritual spring lasted more than a year, but the summer that followed lasted but a week before I was thrust back into autumn. Likewise, just as we experience a day of warm temperatures in the midst of winter, so too can we experience a day of reprieve in the midst of our darkest seasons. And in the midst of summer, a cold spell may drive us inside.

Just as the weatherman tries to predict the weather and misses, we too misread the patterns and get it wrong. We find ourselves unprepared—for we expected one thing and got another. Wisdom tells us to live each day to its fullest. And we must—even as we anticipate the change of autumn, the cold of winter, and the unpredictability of spring. No matter which season we find ourselves in, we must embrace it. Just as we dress for the weather— layers, down coats, raincoats, umbrellas, tank tops, and breathable cottons—we must be prepared. Expect the unexpected. Watch the butterfly. Learn. Live the season you are in. Wait.

Digging Deeper into Spiritual Seasons

Singer and songwriter Nichole Nordeman has written a song that beautifully articulates the spiritual seasons of our lives, called "Every Season.[10]" I'm not sure if she read Parker Palmer's work before she set these lyrics down but it wonderfully parallels his thoughts. It speaks of summer's celebration, autumn's change, winter's slumber, and spring's brave surfacing. It reminds us that we too are being made new, being re-created, through the seasons of our lives.

Before we begin these Bible studies, won't you listen to Nordeman's song? Meditate on the words as you listen. Each verse teaches us more of the spiritual seasons of our lives. Then ask yourself this question:

God's Creative Gift—Unleashing the Artist in You

What season am I in?

Do you know? Study each season again. Where do you find yourself? As you read the following devotions, look at your own spiritual landscape and let it help you determine your season. Dig into your current season. Recall previous seasons of your life and the lessons you learned in each one.

How is God "re-creating" you in the current season of your life?

Digging Deeper: Seasons in the Life of the Artist

Nehemiah 12: Summer's Celebration

John 12:12–50: Autumn's Change

Hosea 6:1–3: Winter's Disorientation

Song of Songs 2: Spring's Singing

Psalm 1: Sitting in Your Season

Digging Deeper:
Summer's Celebration

Read: Nehemiah 12

his passage appears near the end of the book of Nehemiah. It is a story of great celebration and joy. The majority of Nehemiah is focused on the rebuilding of the walls of Jerusalem, the Holy City, following the return of the Israelites from exile. *That* story was spring for the nation of Israel, but *this* story is summer! The remnant has returned, and Nehemiah and Ezra have led the people and worked diligently to restore the walls as foretold by the prophet Isaiah:

> Your people will rebuild the ancient ruins and will raise up the
> age-old foundations; you will be called Repairer of Broken Walls,
> Restorer of Streets with Dwellings. (Isa 58:12)

This celebration has been a long time coming. The exile was their winter. The rebuilding of both the temple and the walls of the city was their spring. They have confessed their sins before God, and he has renewed his covenant with his people (chapter 9)—all part of the preparation of spring as they pushed through the frozen ground of their exile. It is now time for summer's celebration.

Verse 27 contains several key words or phrases. It reads: "At the dedication of the wall of Jerusalem, the Levites were sought out from where they lived and were brought to Jerusalem to celebrate joyfully the dedication with songs of thanksgiving and with the music of cymbals, harps and lyres." The Hebrew word for "to celebrate" is *asah*, and it is also used to describe God's creative activity. All the people are brought together, with God as their head, to celebrate and rejoice. There is a "re-creation" taking place here—a new beginning—and the people come together to celebrate their rebirth.

The Hebrew word for "dedication" is *hanukkah*. It marks the reestablishment of the Israel nation's worship following their exile. There are two large choirs marching around the broad top of the wall of Jerusalem giving thanks and praise, surrounding the city with songs of praise. The Hebrew word used for both the songs of thanksgiving and the choirs assembled to give thanks throughout this passage is *todah*, which is an offering of praise and thanksgiving lifted up as a sacrifice to God (or a choir organized to do so). There is a plurality in its meaning—many voices and/or hands raised in adoration and celebration of what God, the Great Restorer, has done. In fact, their songs of celebration are so loud that they can be heard from miles away!

Lead by the priests and Levites in opposite directions, they meet at the temple area for more thanksgiving and sacrifice. The temple had been desecrated during their time of exile, but they have returned to reclaim and restore it (this occurred earlier and is recorded in the book of Ezra). They offer sacrifices and here in the temple returned to its people; they celebrate what God has accomplished. A great multitude has gathered from near and far to join in this celebration. And yet every person matters—many are mentioned by name. These people had specific roles and their names are mentioned, not just as a matter of record, but to demonstrate that God's specific tasks for them were important and were to be carried out to completion. The women and children, who are rarely included due to their lack of importance in ancient society, are even mentioned: "And on that day they offered great sacrifices, rejoicing because God had given them great joy. The women and children also rejoiced. The sound of rejoicing in Jerusalem could be heard far away" (12:43).

This story illustrates summer. As the people spent years restoring the temple and several more months rebuilding the walls around it, they were working through their season of spring. All has been restored, and they know beyond a shadow of a doubt that summer has finally arrived. No more questions or doubting. Just celebration. Ironically in chapter 13 we find the people of Israel slipping back into their old habits, but Nehemiah is quick to remind the people of their covenant and to right their wrongful ways. There's no way Nehemiah is letting these people drag him back prematurely into winter!

The prophet Amos also writes of this time of restoration:

> "In that day I will restore David's fallen shelter—I will repair its broken walls and restore its ruins—and will rebuild it as it used to be, . . . and I will bring my people Israel back from exile. They will rebuild the ruined cities and live in them. They will plant vineyards and drink their wine; they will make gardens and eat their fruit. I will plant Israel in their own land, never again to be uprooted from the land I have given them," says the LORD your God. (Amos 9:11, 14–15)

Notice the imagery of vineyards and wine. Throughout Scripture, vineyards and wine are meant to remind God's people of blessing and abundance. Read Christ's words found in John 15:1–17. "I am the true vine," Christ teaches us. "Remain in me, as I remain in you." God wants us to remain in this beautiful season of summer, this season of blessing and abundance. But if we fall away, as we so often do, he will prune us back and take us into other seasons meant to help us grow and produce fruit.

Do you remember the warnings of summer?

Don't forget who brought you here into this season.

Share out of the abundant blessings he has given you. Your fruit is meant to be given to others. When you abide in him you will have more than enough to give away.

"I have told you this so that my joy may be in you and that your joy may be complete," Christ tells us. He wants us to be happy, to celebrate, to rejoice. Our joy is only complete in him. If you are in a season of summer, celebrate! Draw close to the source of your joy. Give thanks and praise. Let your voice rise and be heard from miles away. Let your joy overflow and remind others that *summer is real* and indeed possible.

During their time of preparation, Nehemiah said to the people, "Go and enjoy choice food and sweet drinks, and send some to those who have nothing prepared. This day is holy to our Lord. Do not grieve, for the joy of the LORD is your strength" (8:10). Nehemiah's words are words of blessing—summer blessing. Summer is a time to enjoy, to share, to give holy reverence to the Lord, and to let his joy be your strength.

Lord, you have blessed us both richly and deeply. We are amazed at your abundant grace, love, and mercy. We celebrate all that has come before in our lives, all that is in this very moment, and all that is to come. We give you thanks and praise *for* all things and *in* all things. You are the Source of all we have. Let us not hoard our blessings but give them to others in need. Show us who needs the blessing of summer each and every day. May our words speak life and hope to others who are in seasons of darkness and dryness. Open our eyes to all that is around us. We celebrate all that you have given us and all that you are. You are our Summer, Lord. We thank you. We praise you. We give you all the glory! May we be blessed and so also, be a blessing.

In your blessed Name we pray, amen.

Listen to: "Procession of the Levites/Anthem of Praise"
by Richard Smallwood

Digging Deeper:
Autumn's Change

Read: John 12:12–50

his passage signals Christ's transition from summer to autumn. After several years in ministry, he has entered Jerusalem on a donkey with people shouting his praise. "Blessed is he who comes in the name of the Lord!" the people yell. Yet amidst the praise, he knows his hour has come.

The Greek word for "hour" here in verse 23 is *hora*. It marks the end of one time period and the beginning of another. It is used figuratively to represent a season of life. His statement here is a declarative statement. The phrase "has come" is in the perfect tense, which indicates that this is a crucial point in the story. In literary terms, this would signal the turning point of the story. From here on out, Christ's destiny is pointed towards the cross on the hill of Golgotha. There is no turning back.

Yet you can hear his confidence in God. His soul is troubled, yet his faith does not waver. He understands that in death, there is life—not for him alone, but for all! The single seed dies so that it can produce more fruit. Christ clearly states, "It was for this very reason I came to this hour." He knows his purpose, his destiny, and he is ready to fulfill it, no matter the cost.

Then in verse 28 we hear God's voice from heaven. This is the third and final time in the Gospel accounts we hear a voice from heaven. The first time is found in the other three Gospels when Christ is baptized. The Spirit descends like a dove, and we hear the voice of God say, "This is my beloved son, with whom I am well pleased" (Matt 3:16–17; Mark 1:11; Luke 3:22). Christ's identity is secured in God who loves him and is pleased with him. He fulfills his ministry's purpose and is brought to this moment. His obedience never fails to astound me.

In *The Dance of Life*, Nouwen writes:

> Jesus shows, both in his teachings and in his life, that true joy often is hidden in the midst of our sorrow, and that the dance of life finds its beginnings in grief. He says: "Unless the grain of wheat dies, it cannot bear fruit . . . Unless we lose our lives, we cannot find them; unless the Son of Man dies, he cannot send the spirit."
>
> . . . Here a completely new way of living is revealed. It is the way in which pain can be embraced, not out of a desire to suffer, but in the knowledge that something new will be born in the pain.[11]

Can we embrace change, uncertainty, and pain the way Jesus teaches? If we are to be made into the image of Christ, it is our calling. But do we have the guts to walk in it? This can be a time of great discovery of your identity and worth. You need to continually ask yourself:

What am I learning?
What is God asking me to let go of?
What does this have to do with my identity in him?
How does this help God fulfill his destiny in my life?
Can I hear God's voice from heaven?

What is your loss? What changes are you facing right now in your spiritual autumn? Write it down. Give it to God. Cry. Let go. I stated this earlier, but it bears repeating: *The heart cannot let go of that which it has not grieved.* Let your spirit grieve its losses. Christ teaches us that unless we lose our lives, we cannot find them. This process requires great honesty with yourself and with God. Who are you trusting? God? Yourself? You will only trust God to the degree that you know you are loved by Him. God is *for* you (Rom 8:31) and *with* you (Matt 1:23). Do you believe that? Truly believe that? And are you ready to let go and let God?

Remember the dance of travail? This might be a good time to dance it. In an Advent meditation called "Waiting with Mary," Isaac Villegas tells us, "To have faith is to know that God waits with us. To have faith is to recognize that this laborious waiting is the coming of God. Our travail is the coming of God. We are overflowing with God, whether we believe it or not. God's new life is always about to happen, even when it seems impossible."[12]

As I write this devotion, I have just entered a spiritual season of autumn. Ironically, my foot is hurt in such a way that I cannot dance. The very way God has asked me to travail in the past is the very thing he is asking me to let go of. So I must learn a new dance of travail. Perhaps it is the book you hold in your hands? I've spent a long time in the writing process. I start, I stop, I start again. Life gets in the way, and I am pulled away yet again. Yet God is asking me to travail—to write in the promises of a dream and a destiny fulfilled. I can no longer avoid this calling, this creative process, this dance of travail. Despite my loss, I am filled with excitement and joy. Do I have my bad days? Certainly! But I look to my God for wisdom, discernment, and reassurance. My heart's song in this season is "God I look to You" by Jenn Johnson.[13] It reminds me that my God reigns above all in heaven and earth—nothing can conquer his love for me and his power over the things of this earth.

Father God, like Christ, we make a declarative statement: Our God reigns! We look the enemy square in the face and declare that the God of heaven and earth reigns over every situation in our lives! We take back all he has threatened to steal from us and declare that you, O God, are powerful and sovereign in all situations. We declare you as ruler over all things in heaven and earth.

In your powerful Name we pray, amen.

Listen to: "God I Look to You" by Jenn Johnson

Digging Deeper:
Winter's Disorientation

Read: Hosea 6:1–3

As we have noted before, the book of Hosea speaks of God's covenantal love for his people. As an ultimate symbolic act, the prophet Hosea takes a prostitute as his wife, and his marriage becomes a symbol of the relationship between Yahweh and his wayward wife, Israel. Over and over the prophet calls his people to *return* to, *acknowledge*, and *know* their God. And here in this passage we find the renewal and resurrection of God's covenant with his people.[14] Although Hosea is speaking to his own nation, this prophetic passage reaches far into the future. According to Bible scholar Douglas Stuart, "Its orientation is eschatological, not immediate."[15] That means it speaks to a *future* state of God's kingdom *here on earth*. He continues, "The fulfillment of the [passage] is thus implicitly reserved for another generation."[16]

I believe that the fulfillment of this passage is found in the new covenant of Christ's blood—spilled in atonement for the sins of all people. The significance of the "two days/third day" echoes back to God's original covenant established at Mt. Sinai (Exod 19:11, 15)[17] and looks forward to a new covenant established by Christ's shed blood (1 Cor 15:4). The phrase "raise up" here is the Hebrew word *qum*, and it is used other places in Scripture to refer to the coming Messiah of the nation of Israel (Num 24:17; Deut 18:15; Jer 23:5). If Hosea's marriage symbolizes the old covenant between God and Israel, then the future fulfillment is found in the new covenant established between Christ and his bride, the church, when he laid down his life so that we might also be raised up with him.

And this brings us to the ultimate purpose of the spiritual season of winter in our lives: winter brings the death of our old self so the new self can emerge (Col 3:1–10). If we are to follow in the footsteps of Christ, we too must crucify our old, sinful nature. Galatians 2:19–20 states: "I have been crucified with Christ. It is no longer I who live, but Christ who lives in me. And the life I now live in the flesh I live by faith in the Son of God, who loved me and gave himself for me."

Think of the symbols of winter—
the barren tree, the dormant bulb, and the butterfly's chrysalis.
All seems quiet, still, dead, like nothing's happening.

Yet these symbols remind us that within that quiet stillness,
great change is taking place!

Many great spiritual writers—from the ancient to the quite modern—have written about the important place of silence and solitude in our spiritual lives. One of those is Henri Nouwen. In his book *The Dance of Life*, he writes:

> Solitude is the garden for our hearts which yearn for love. It is the place where our aloneness can bear fruit. . . . It is not an easy place to be, since we are so insecure and fearful that we are easily distracted by whatever promises immediate satisfaction. Solitude is not immediately satisfying, because in solitude we meet our demons, our addictions, our feelings of lust and anger, and our immense need for recognition and approval. But if we do not run away, we will meet there also the One who says; "Do not be afraid. I am with you, and I will guide you through the valley of darkness."[18]

He also asks this poignant question: "Does not all creativity ask for a certain encounter with loneliness, and does not the fear of this encounter severely limit our possible self expression?"[19]

What do these insights teach us? Solitude is necessary for our growth—as believers and as artists. It helps us confront those things that need to be crucified with Christ. It helps us find our true center—our "due north." It keeps us from earthly distraction. It helps us develop our creative spirit.

Consider the symbolism of baptism for a moment. In baptism we are thrust under the water and brought back up to symbolize our death and resurrection with Christ. We are buried—all our sin, shame, guilt, and misguided intentions pulled into the grave with Christ. A moment later we are pulled from the depths of our depravity to new life—resurrection life in the Spirit through the power of Christ who conquered sin and death and hell!

Our solitude is the same. In the silence of our winter's grave, we are brought face to face with all that pulls us down in order to bury it as we die to our old, false selves. Then we are raised from that grave as a new creation in Christ: "Therefore, if anyone is in Christ, he is a new creation. The old has passed away; behold, the new has come!" (2 Cor 5:17)

For those who have experienced immersion baptism, there is this moment in the process of being pushed underwater where you can become disoriented. In my tradition we practice triune immersion—we are dunked three times in the name of the Father, Son, and Holy Spirit. You must rely on your baptizer to dunk and pull you back up, not once, but *three* times! Each time you experience this disorientation, you learn to trust your baptizer a little bit more.

This same disorientation happens during the winter of your soul. You're not quite sure which way is up or forward, but in the process you learn to trust God more. Kidd writes of a sermon she once heard on the "dark night" of the soul: "The minister pointed out that the most significant events in Jesus' life took place in darkness: his birth, his arrest, his death, his resurrection. His point was that although darkness in the spiritual life has gotten a lot of bad press, it sometimes yields extraordinary events."[20]

In Isaiah 45:3, God promises: "I will give you treasures hidden in the darkness—secret riches. I will do this so you may know that I am the Lord, the God of Israel, the one who calls you by name." In this place of death, disorientation, darkness, and disintegration, God gives us secret riches. If only we would have the heart to stay, dig deep, and mine them!

There is so much more I could write about this subject. I encourage you to find the resources that will help you navigate this season. The following is a short list of the many resources that have greatly encouraged me during the winter seasons in my life:

- Carol Kent, *When I Lay My Isaac Down: Unshakeable Faith in Unthinkable Circumstances* (Colorado Springs, CO: NavPress, 2004)

- Sue Monk Kidd, *When the Heart Waits: Spiritual Direction for Life's Sacred Questions* (New York: Harper & Row, 1990)

- Anne Graham Lotz, *Why? Trusting God When You Don't Understand* (Nashville: W Publishing, 2004)

- Henri J. M. Nouwen, *The Dance of Life: Weaving Sorrows and Blessings into One Joyful Step* (Notre Dame, IN: Ave Maria, 2005)

- Nicol Sponberg, "Resurrection" (Curb Records, 2004). The lyrics of this song perfectly express the loss of this season. There are two dances on YouTube that beautifully portray the death of the false self and resurrection into new life. One is danced by Praise in Motion and the other by Selah Warriors. Both are poignant examples of how creative expression helps others through the seasons of their lives.

- Terry Wardle, *Draw Close to the Fire: Finding God in the Darkness* (Siloam Springs, AR: Leafwood, 2004)

Let us return once more to our Hosea passage. Do you see the hope that lies within? Hosea speaks as one who trusts in the Lord's sovereignty with conviction and faith. The sun and the rain are two things that are both predictable and certain. The NIV translation words it this way: "As surely as the sun rises, he will appear" (6:3b).

Lord Jesus, help me to know that you will appear, yes, as surely as the sun rises! I trust you Lord to make my winter into something beautiful. Crucify my false self and resurrect me into my new self—a new creation found in Christ's atoning work of the cross and resurrection. I humbly submit to this process and look forward in hope and joy to all that you have for me in the next season of my life.

In the Name of he who makes all things new, Jesus, amen.

Listen to: "Resurrection" by Nicol Sponberg

Digging Deeper:
Spring's Singing

Read: Song of Songs 2

his passage has much to say to those who are emerging from winter into spring. It paints a beautiful picture with its imagery and calls us to a season of song. While there are several interpretations of the Song of Songs, for our purposes here, let us interpret this as the voice of our Lover (Christ Jesus) calling out to his Beloved (his church, and more specifically, *you*).

Reread verses 10–13. This short passage is written as a *chiasm*. As you may recall, this means it begins and ends in a similar way with the most important words being in the middle: "the season of singing has come" (v. 12a). The specific word in the very middle is "singing," which is the Hebrew word *zamir*, which also means "harvest."[21] The winter has past, and it is time to reap a harvest from all that the heart has endured through the still-ness of winter and the harshness of the early spring rains. Spring has come, and Christ calls his beloved to sing his praises!

As the Lover speaks we find his dove hiding (v. 14). To understand this fully you must understand the imagery from the writer's context. Biblical scholar Richard Hess reports that there were two places in Palestine where thousands of doves nested in the rocky clefts of the mountains. The struc-ture of these lines implies that the beloved is inaccessible—hidden away.[22] God indeed is our hiding place, our refuge, and our rock. However, he also calls us from those hiding places in him—calling us to awaken our spirits, to join him in the harvest, and to sing praises in the season of spring!

Later in the Song of Songs, the Beloved tells us: "I slept, but my heart was awake. A sound! My beloved is knocking. 'Open to me, my sister, my love, my dove, my perfect one'" (5:2). Revelation paints this same picture of Christ knocking and calling out for his beloved: "Behold, I stand at the door and knock. If anyone hears my voice and opens the door, I will come in to him and eat with him, and he with me" (3:20). Notice Christ, the lover of our souls, waiting to be let in. Could he barge in if he wanted to? Yes, but like a true gentleman, he knocks, he waits, and he gently calls out to us. We choose if we respond. Will we keep ourselves hidden away in the quiet recesses of our hearts, or will we throw open the door and let him in?

After a particularly long season of winter, my friend Terry was praying for me. "I get a sense of a 'slumbering spirit' within you," he said. In the midst of the harshness of winter, as I buried myself away for protection from the elements, my spirit had entered a hibernation of sorts. God's voice had been inaudible for so long that my ears couldn't hear his voice calling out to me. My spirit had fallen into a deep sleep, and it was having trouble waking up again! Yet God was calling me forth. Was I going to answer, to respond to my lover's voice, or would I stay hidden away? It took definite perseverance and strength, but I eventually chose to respond. Everything in me wanted to crawl back under the covers, back into the hidden places deep within my spirit. My spirit needed a double shot of espresso to waken from the long, harsh winter of my soul!

Just as the Lover calls his Beloved to sing in this passage from Song of Songs, so too does God call us to sing! Can you hear his voice calling out to you to sing, to dance, to rejoice? Taste the breakthrough! Open wide your arms, your spirit, your heart so the King of Glory might come in!

> Open up, ancient gates!
> Open up, ancient doors, and let the King of glory enter.
> Who is the King of glory?
> The Lord, strong and mighty; the Lord, invincible in battle.
> Open up, ancient gates!
> Open up, ancient doors, and let the King of glory enter.
> Who is the King of glory?
> The Lord of Heaven's Armies—he is the King of glory.
> (Ps 24:7–10 , NLT)

The King of Glory in all his splendor is waiting for you. Will you open up those ancient gates, long shut off from his majesty and glory?

What does your song of spring sound like, look like, feel like? The Lover of your soul is calling out to you: "Let me see your face; let me hear your voice." What face will you put to your praise? What lyrics will you set down to sing to him? How can your art form give life to your slumbering spirit? Is there a project you have long tucked away for another day? Perhaps he is calling you to bring it back out, to resurrect it, so that he can breathe new life into it?

In spring, winter's death is swallowed up in the resurrection victory, promising new life (1 Cor 15:54). Respond to his voice; answer his knock; acknowledge your lover beckoning to you. Still struggling to wake from your slumber? Cry out to him to breakthrough with you. Micah 2:13 says,

"The One who breaks open the way will go up before you; together, you will break through the gate and go out. Your King will pass through before you, the LORD at your head" (paraphrase). The One who breaks through before you is beckoning you to follow!

Christ Jesus, you are indeed the King of Glory! You are the Lord of Hosts, who breaks through the ancient gates in our lives! We respond to your voice in song and dance, taking in the beauty of the spring season before us. Remove the scales from our eyes; help us to see you in every blossom and bud! Remove the wax from our ears; help us hear you in every bird's song! Awaken our taste buds; help us savor you in the freshness of the spring rains! We awaken our hearts to all that you have for us. Lord, where our spirit's struggle to awaken, help us to persevere until we are fully awake to your beauty and love. You are the Lover of our souls; we are your beloved.

In the Name of he who calls us from the grave, amen.

Listen to: "Slumber" by NEEDTOBREATHE

Digging Deeper:
Sitting in Your Season

Read: Psalm 1

Like many Bible passages, this passage makes use of metaphor to illustrate a life lived in fellowship with God, in obedience to his law. It opens the book of Psalms, and lays down the tenet through which God's people join together in worship. Whereas the rest of the Psalms read as worship, this reads more like Proverbs; in fact, when you first read it you might think that you accidentally skipped over Psalms. However, this is no accident—this piece of wisdom opens the Psalms and sets the stage for all that follows.

Another similar metaphor is found in Jeremiah 17:7–8: "Blessed is the man who trusts in the LORD, whose trust is the LORD. He is like a tree planted by water, that sends out its roots by the stream, and does not fear when heat comes, for its leaves remain green, and is not anxious in the year of drought, for it does not cease to bear fruit." Both use the tree to illustrate a particular type of relationship with God.

While the passage in Psalms is clear that this kind of life is only available to those who delight in and meditate on the law of the Lord, the Jeremiah passage promises this kind of life to the one who trusts in the Lord. Although they express two different things, they are, of course, related. One cannot trust someone they don't know, and we know God by meditating on his word. Those who follow his word—the law, with its constructs, parameters, and traditions—trust in God for they see his way is good and leads to a life blessed by him. In both passages the tree becomes our symbol. However, before we look at the tree, let us look to where it is planted—where it receives its sustenance.

This tree is planted by water—its source of life. Throughout Scripture, there are many references to water and thirst. The psalmist writes, "O God, you are my God; earnestly I seek you; my soul thirsts for you; my flesh faints for you, as in a dry and weary land where there is no water" (Ps 63:1). Humans are born with a natural thirst—not just a physical thirst, but also an internal thirst. We were created with this inborn craving to drive us to our "true source." While many people, Christians and non-Christians alike, drink from broken cisterns (Jer 2:13) and stagnant ponds, there is a better source—a source of Living Water that is available to all who seek.

The prophet Isaiah spoke of the promise of this Living Water:

> When the poor and needy search for water and there is none,
> and their tongues are parched from thirst,
> then I, the Lord, will answer them.
> I, the God of Israel, will never forsake them.
> I will open up rivers for them on high plateaus.
> I will give them fountains of water in the valleys.
> In the deserts they will find pools of water.
> Rivers fed by springs will flow across the dry, parched ground.
> I will plant trees…on barren land.
> Everyone will see this miracle and understand that it is the Lord,
> the Holy One of Israel, who did it. (Isa 41:17–20, NLT)

This promise was fulfilled in the Incarnation of God in Jesus Christ, who offered water "that takes away thirst altogether. It becomes a perpetual spring within [us], giving [us] eternal life" (John 4:14, NLT). Isaiah also prophesied that this Living Water would flow upon Israel's descendants as the Spirit of the Living God (Isa 44:3), and we see the fulfillment of this through the coming of the promised Holy Spirit in Acts 2. So, we see this Living Water as triune in nature—promised by God, brought to earth by Christ, and poured out through the Holy Spirit.

Jesus said, "If you only knew the gift God has for you and who I am, you would ask me, and I would give you living water" (John 4:10, NLT). How many people live dry, barren lives because they do not know the gift that he offers each and every one of us? How many people bear no fruit in ministry? "If anyone is thirsty, let him come to me and drink. Whoever believes in me, as the scripture has said, streams of living water will flow from within him" (John 7:37–38). As we partake of this water, we become like willows or poplars that spring up by the watercourses (Isa 44:4, AMP) and life flows in and through us.

What does it mean to be a like a tree? A tree is anchored and supported by large roots that spread out below the ground. When the wind comes, trees with healthy root systems stay anchored, while trees with weak or damaged roots fall to the ground. In addition, these larger roots send out tiny, feeder roots that absorb water and nutrients from the soil. Just as a tree sends out its roots to survive and to thrive, we must also be deeply rooted in God and his word. When the winds of change begin to blow in our lives do we fall or are we unmovable and anchored in God?

In the second letter to Timothy, Paul instructs him to "be prepared in season and out of season" (2:4a). A tree doesn't bear its fruit in all four seasons of the year. Each season has its purpose in the seasonal cycles of the tree. Even in winter, when it looks as though the tree is dead, it is not. The tree is hibernating through the harshness of winter, when the days are shorter and the temperatures are below freezing. We too must be anchored deeply in God to weather the cycles of our spiritual seasons.

I titled this devotion "Sitting in Your Season" because I know how difficult it is to actually "sit" in the seasons of our lives. I struggled with this study for weeks because frankly I am not very good at sitting in my season. I am both impatient *and* complacent! In my impatience, I look ahead to the next season and want to uproot myself and move on, forgetting to do the work of the season I am in. And because God doesn't like me to get ahead of him, he pulls me back into waiting and then my complacency sets in. In my complacency, I get lazy and forget that there is work to do in this season. I slough it off, leaving it for another day, and find that it never gets done—at least to God's satisfaction!

Each season has its preparation—the things that need done before we can move on. The farmer orders his seeds in winter to prepare for the coming season. And if he doesn't? Well then he has nothing to plant come spring. Our spiritual lives are the same. If we don't sit in our season and do the work required there, then when we move on we find ourselves unprepared for our current situation. In the end, God takes us back to repeat the cycle until we finally get it right. He's very patient that way. And he does want us to get it right. God wants us to experience the fullness of each season. To be prepared at all times.

Whether our ministry is bearing fruit or not has a lot to do with the preparation of previous seasons. If we have uprooted ourselves from beside streams of Living Water, we have no reserves to operate and find ourselves dry and our fruit withers and falls to the ground to rot.

> *Is that the picture you have for your life? Your ministry?*
> *Withered and rotting fruit on the ground?*

If you find yourself stagnated in your season, I encourage you to return to the stream of Living Water; to return to God's word; to return to your True Source. Challenge yourself to not move ahead until you have completed the work of this season. Cry out to God to show you the work and preparation he requires of you and your ministry. And don't give up until he has answered. And once he's answered, listen to his voice, his instruction.

God of the Seasons, I pray that you will give each of us the patience and endurance to sit in our current season. That we will not grow weary or bored. That we will be able to see with spiritual insight the preparation that is required in this very moment so that you can move us forward. I pray that we will each be like trees rooted deeply by streams of Living Water and that we will draw our sustenance from him.

I pray that if we are in *summer,*
we will be generous with our fruit
and the many blessings he has poured upon us.

I pray that if we are in *fall,*
we will drop our leaves with grace and beauty,
preparing for the season to come.

I pray that if we are in *winter,*
we will rest under the blanket of pure white peace
that falls around us.

I pray that if we are in *spring,*
we will thrust through the once solid ground
to find a world of glorious Sonshine.

I pray these things in the Name of he who orders the seasons,
our Creator God, Amen.

Listen to: "Tree" by Justin Rizzo

Endnotes

1. Brown, "Ecclesiastes," 41.

2. Palmer, *Let Your Life Speak*. All material is taken from chapter 6: "There Is a Season," 95ff.

3. Ibid., 106.

4. Ibid., 108.

5. Ibid., 98.

6. Kidd, *When the Heart Waits*. I *highly recommend* this book for anyone experiencing winter. My pastor gave me this book during a very long winter of my spirit and it stayed with my Bible the entire time. I literally read parts of it over and over until the season had finally passed. Based on the metaphor of the butterfly and its chrysalis, the book guides you through the places of deep discovery. See Isaiah 45:3.

7. Ibid., 17.

8. Palmer, *Let Your Life Speak*. 109.

9. Kidd, *When the Heart Waits*, 13.

10. Nichole Nordeman, "Every Season" (Ariose Music, admin. by EMI Christian Music, 2000).

11. Nouwen, *Dance of Life*, 163–64.

12. Villegas, "Waiting with Mary."

13. Jenn Johnson and Ian Mcintosh, "God I Look to You" (Bethel Music, 2010).

14. Yee, "Hosea," 250.

15. Stuart, *Hosea*, 107.

16. Ibid., 108.

17. Yee, "Hosea," 250.

18. Nouwen, *Dance of Life*, 72–73.

19. Ibid., 94.

20. Kidd, *When the Heart Waits*, 151. The concept of the "dark night of the soul" was the work of St. John of the Cross, a sixteenth-century Carmelite priest. It was written while he was imprisoned by his own Carmelite brothers for his attempts to reform their order.

21. Hess, *Song of Songs*, 92.

22. Ibid., 95–96. We find the same imagery in Jeremiah 48:28 as well.

Appendix: Symbolic Acts of the Prophets

1 Kings 11:29-39 — Ahijah tears his cloak in twelve strips and gives ten to Jeroboam.

> **Meaning:** God will tear the kingdom of Israel from Solomon and give ten tribes to Jeroboam to rule over.

1 Kings 22:10-11 — Zedekiah made iron horns for kings of Judah and Israel.

> **Meaning:** The kings will gore the Arameans.

2 Kings 13:14-19 — Elisha tells King Jehoash to shoot and strike the ground with arrows.

> **Meaning:** The Lord's arrow of victory. By striking the ground three times, he will defeat his enemy only three times because he did not go far enough.

Nehemiah 5:13 — Nehemiah shakes out his robes.

> **Meaning:** God will shake out and empty anyone who did not keep his promise to help the poor and oppressed.

Isaiah 7:3 & 8:1-4 — Naming of Isaiah's children.

> **Meaning:** Shear-Jashub means "a remnant will return" and Maher-Shalal-Hash-Baz means "quick to the plunder, swift to the spoil," which foretold the plundering of Damascus and Samaria.

Isaiah 20:1-6 — Isaiah strips himself of his loincloth and sandals for three years.

> **Meaning:** Egyptian and Cushite captives will be lead away naked and barefoot by the king of Assyria.

Jeremiah 13:1–11 — Jeremiah buys, wears, and then buries a linen belt.

> **Meaning:** Ruined belt is God ruining the pride of Judah and Jerusalem.

Jeremiah 16:1–9 — God forbids Jeremiah to marry, have children, and attend funeral observations or feasts.

> **Meaning:** In the fall of Israel, women and children will die, no one will mourn for them, and the sounds of joy will be no more.

Jeremiah 18:1–12 — Jeremiah observes marred pottery being remade at a potter's house.

> **Meaning:** God will reform the marred house of Israel.

Jeremiah 19:1–15 — Jeremiah smashes the pottery at the Potsherd Gate.

> **Meaning:** God will smash Judah beyond repair.

Jeremiah 27:1–28:17 — Jeremiah wears a wooden yoke. Hananiah breaks it.

> **Meaning:** Judah will live under the yoke of Babylon. After Hananiah (false prophet) breaks the yoke, Jeremiah prophesied that he would wear an iron yoke and later that year Hananiah dies.

Jeremiah 32:1–44 — Jeremiah buys a field at Anathoth.

> **Meaning:** Although the Lord has brought disaster to his people, he will restore their land and their fortunes.

Jeremiah 35:1–19 — Jeremiah sets wine before faithful Recabites who won't drink it.

> **Meaning:** The Recabites set an example to the people of Judah and Jerusalem of obedience. The Israelites are to follow this example.

Jeremiah 43:8–13 — Jeremiah buries large stones at the entrance of Pharaoh's palace.

> **Meaning:** God will set the throne of Nebuchadnezar, king of Babylon, over the place where these stones were buried, and he will defeat the Egyptians and rule over them.

Jeremiah 51:59-64 — Jeremiah asks Seraiah to throw a scroll with a stone attached into the river after reading it to the people of Babylon.

Meaning: Babylon will sink and not rise again.

Ezekiel 4:1-17 & 5:1-4 — Ezekiel does a series of actions, including lying on his side while prophesying and shaving his beard.

Meaning: This series of actions represent the coming siege of Jerusalem.

Ezekiel 12:1-16 — Ezekiel packs his baggage as an exile.

Meaning: The people of Jerusalem will go into exile as captives.

Ezekiel 12:17-20 — Ezekiel trembles as he eats and drinks.

Meaning: The people will eat their food in anxiety and drink their water in despair.

Ezekiel 21:6-7 — Ezekiel is to groan before the people.

Meaning: Groaning represents God's grief and how every heart will be broken in the coming day of judgment.

Ezekiel 21:14-17 — Ezekiel is to strike his hands together as he prophesies.

Meaning: The sword of judgment will strike Judah; then God will strike his hands together to end the judgment.

Ezekiel 24:15-27 — Ezekiel is not to mourn his wife's death.

Meaning: God will desecrate his temple and the people will be unable to mourn.

Ezekiel 37:15-23 — Ezekiel holds two sticks together as one.

Meaning: Judah and Israel will be reunited as one nation with one king to rule over them.

Hosea 1:2-11 — Hosea takes a wife of whoredom and names his children symbolically.

Meaning: God loves the adulteress nation of Israel. The names of the children represent the judgment and subsequent restoration of Israel.

Hosea 3:1–5 — Hosea redeems his wife from adultery and slavery.

> **Meaning:** God loves his people even though they are unfaithful. Israel will return to seek God.

Zechariah 6:9–15 — Zechariah makes a crown of silver and gold to crown Joshua.

> **Meaning:** Joshua will rebuild the temple and rule over the nation as a priest.

Zechariah 11:4–7 — Zechariah acts as shepherd and then names and breaks two staffs.

> **Meaning:** God will raise up a shepherd who will not care for the flock of Israel. The broken staffs represent God breaking his covenant with his people.

Acts 21:10–15 — The prophet Agabus binds the hands and feet of Paul.

> **Meaning:** Paul will be bound by the people of Jerusalem and handed over to the Gentiles.

Bibliography

Atchison, Doug, writer and director. *Akeelah and the Bee*. Lions Gate, 2006.

Batz, Jeannette. "Embodying Praise." *National Catholic Reporter* 35/6 (December 4, 1998). Online: http://natcath.org/NCR_Online/archives2/1998d/120498t.htm.

Begbie, Jeremy S. *Voicing Creation's Praise: Towards a Theology of the Arts*. Eugene, OR: Wipf & Stock, 2003.

Best, Harold M. *Unceasing Worship: Biblical Perspectives on Worship and the Arts*. Downers Grove, IL: InterVarsity, 2003.

Blenkinsopp, Joseph. *Ezekiel*. Interpretation. Louisville: John Knox, 1990.

Brown, Raymond. *The Message of Numbers*. The Bible Speaks Today. Downers Grove, IL: InterVarsity, 2002.

Brown, William P. *Ecclesiastes*. Interpretation. Louisville: John Knox, 2000.

Butler, Stephanie. *My Body Is the Temple: Encounters and Revelations of Sacred Dance and Artistry*. Fairfax, VA: Xulon, 2002.

Chen, Pat. *The Depths of God: Walking Ancient Paths into His Presence*. Shippensburg, PA: Destiny Image, 2003.

Clark, Heather. *The Dancing Hand of God*. Self-published, Canada, 2007.

Craigie, Peter C. *Psalms 1–50*. 2nd ed. Word Biblical Commentary 19. Nashville: T. Nelson, 2004.

DeSola, Carla. *The Spirit Moves: Handbook of Dance and Prayer*. Austin: The Sharing Company, 1986.

Douglas–Klotz, Neil. "Ruth St. Denis: Sacred Dance Explorations in America." In *Dance as Religious Studies*, edited by Doug Adams and Diane Apostolos-Cappadona, 109–17. Eugene, OR: Wipf & Stock, 1993.

Duckworth, Penelope. "The Incarnate Word." In *I Am: Teaching Sermons on the Incarnation*, edited by Ronald F. Allen, 39–42. Nashville: Abington, 1998.

Dunn, James D. G. "Incarnation." In *Anchor Bible Dictionary* 3:397–404.

Foster, Richard J. *Streams of Living Water: Celebrating the Great Traditions of Christian Faith*. San Francisco: Harper, 1998.

Fowler, James W. *Becoming Adult, Becoming Christian: Adult Development and Christian Faith*. San Francisco: Jossey-Bass, 2000.

Gire, Ken. *Windows of the Soul*. Grand Rapids: Zondervan, 1996.

Goens, Linda M. *Praising God through the Lively Arts*. Nashville: Abingdon, 1999.

Green, Joel B. *1 Peter*. The Two Horizons New Testament Commentary. Grand Rapids: Eerdmans, 2007.

Gunkel, Hermann. *Genesis*. Translated by Mark E. Biddle. Mercer Library of Biblical Studies. Mason, GA: Mercer University Press, 1997.

Hagner, Donald A. *Matthew 1–13*. Word Biblical Commentary 33A. Dallas: Word, 1993.

Bibliography

Hart, Trevor. "Through the Arts: Hearing, Seeing, and Touching the Truth." In *Beholding the Glory: Incarnation through the Arts*, edited by Jeremy Begbie, 1–26. Grand Rapids: Baker, 2000.

Hebrew-Greek Key Word Study Bible: New International Version. Edited by Spiros Zodhiates. Chattanooga, TN: AMG, 1996.

Herman, Bruce. "Wounds and Beauty." In *The Beauty of God: Theology and the Arts*, edited by Daniel J. Treier, Mark Husbands, and Roger Lundin, 110–20. Downers Grove, IL: InterVarsity, 2007.

Hess, Richard S. *Song of Songs.* Baker Commentary on the Old Testament Wisdom and Psalms. Grand Rapids: Baker, 2005.

Jones, Tony. *The Sacred Way: Spiritual Practices for Everyday Life.* Grand Rapids: Zondervan, 2005.

Kane, Thomas. "Shaping Liturgical Dance." In *Introducing Dance in Christian Worship*, by Ronald Gagne, Thomas Kane, and Robert VerEecke, 86–125. Rev. ed. Portland, OR: Pastoral, 1999.

Kegley, Jacquelyn Ann K. *Paul Tillich on Creativity.* Lanham, MD: University Press of America, 1989.

Kelly, Thomas R. *A Testament of Devotion.* New York: Harper, 1941.

Kidd, Sue Monk. *When the Heart Waits: Spiritual Direction for Life's Sacred Questions.* San Francisco: Harper & Row, 1990.

Kovacs, Aimee Verduzco. *Dancing into the Anointing: Touching the Heart of God through Dance.* Shippensburg, PA: Destiny Image, 1996.

Kuyper, Abraham. *Calvinism.* London: Sovereign Grace Union, 1932.

Lane, William L. *Hebrews 1–8.* Word Biblical Commentary 47A. Dallas: Word, 1991.

Langmead, Ross. *The Word Made Flesh: Towards an Incarnational Missiology.* Lanham, MD: University Press of America, 2004.

L'Engle, Madeleine. *Walking on Water: Reflections on Faith and Art.* Wheaton, IL: H. Shaw, 1980.

Lewis, C. S. *The Last Battle.* New York: Scholastic, 1995.

———. *Mere Christianity.* New York: Macmillan, 1943.

Lindblom, Johannes. *Prophecy in Ancient Israel.* Oxford: Alden, 1962.

Miller, Patrick D. "The Book of Jeremiah." In *The New Interpreter's Bible*, edited by Leander Keck, 6:555–926. Nashville: Abingdon, 2001.

Nouwen, Henri J. M. *The Dance of Life: Weaving Sorrows and Blessings into One Joyful Step.* Edited by Michael Ford. Notre Dame, IN: Ave Maria, 2005.

———. *The Living Reminder: Service and Prayer in Memory of Jesus.* San Francisco: Harper, 1977.

———. *The Wounded Healer: Minisry in Contemporary Society.* London: Darton, Longman and Todd, 1994.

Olson, Dennis T. *Numbers.* Interpretation. Louisville: John Knox, 1996.

Palmer, Parker J. *Let Your Life Speak: Listening for the Voice of Vocation.* San Francisco: Jossey-Bass, 2000.

Peterson, Eugene H. *Christ Plays in Ten Thousand Places: A Conversation in Spiritual Theology.* Grand Rapids: Eerdmans, 2005.

———. *The Message: The Bible in Contemporary Language.* Colorado Springs, CO: NavPress, 2002.

Rognlien, Bob. *Experiential Worship: Encountering God with Heart, Soul, Mind, and Strength.* Colorado Springs, CO: NavPress, 2005.

Sailhamer, John H. "Genesis." In *The Expositor's Bible Commentary with the New International Version*, vol. 2, *Genesis, Exodus, Leviticus, Numbers*, edited by Frank E. Gaebelein. Grand Rapids: Zondervan, 1990.

——. *NIV Compact Bible Commentary*. Grand Rapids: Zondervan, 1994.

St. Denis, Ruth. "The Sword" In *Lotus Light, Poems*. New York: Houghton Mifflin, 1932.

Savage, Sara B. "Through Dance: Fully Human, Fully Alive." In *Beholding the Glory: Incarnation through the Arts*, edited by Jeremy Begbie, 64–82. Grand Rapids: Baker, 2000.

Schmidt, Thomas. *A Scandalous Beauty: The Artistry of God and the Way of the Cross*. Grand Rapids: Brazos, 2002.

Schroeder, Celeste Snowber. *Embodied Prayer: Harmonizing Body and Soul*. Liguori, MO: Triumph, 1995.

Story, Laura. "Story behind the Song: Laura Story's 'Indescribable.'" *CCM Magazine*, May 2008. Online: http://www.ccmmagazine.com/just_for_you/story_behind_the_song/11574719/. Accessed March 2, 2010.

Stuart, Douglas K. *Hosea–Jonah*. Word Biblical Commentary 31. Waco, TX: Word, 1987.

Stubbs, David L. *Numbers*. Brazos Theological Commentary on the Bible. Grand Rapids: Brazos, 2009.

Taylor, Margaret Fisk. *A Time to Dance: Symbolic Movement in Worship*. Philadelphia: United Church Press, 1967.

Thompson, J. A. *The Book of Jeremiah*. New International Commentary on the Old Testament. Grand Rapids: Eerdmans, 1980.

Thompson, Marianne Meye. *The Incarnate Word: Perspectives on Jesus in the Fourth Gospel*. Peabody, MA: Hendrickson, 1988.

VerEecke, Robert. "A Vision of a Dancing Church." In *Introducing Dance in Christian Worship*, by Ronald Gagne, Thomas Kane, and Robert VerEecke, 128–208. Rev. ed. Portland, OR: Pastoral, 1999.

Villegas, Isaac S. "Waiting with Mary: A Meditation on Luke 1:26–38, 47–55." *The Other Journal*, November 29, 2011. Online: http://theotherjournal.com/ 2011/11/29/ waiting-with-mary-a-meditation-on-luke-126-38-47-55/.

Waggoner, Brenda. *Fairy Tale Faith: Living in the Meantime When You Expected Happily Ever After*. Wheaton, IL: Tyndale, 2003.

Williamson, Marianne. *A Return to Love: Reflections on the Principles of A Course in Miracles*. New York: Harper Collins, 1992.

Yee, Gale A. "Hosea." In *The New Interpreter's Bible*, edited by Leander E. Keck, vol. 7. Nashville: Abingdon, 1996.

Zschech, Darlene. *Extravagant Worship*. Castle Hill, NSW, Australia: Check Music Ministries, 2001.